Praises fo  D0877367

My Current Past

Jhiree's commitment to supporting the healing and wellbeing of those in her community and the world is apparent in the rich body of work and service she delivers selflessly. She is a woman who willingly stretches herself beyond what is required or expected, landing in a sphere of ever-expanding excellence. Her impact IS changing the world.

– Sheila Robinson-Kiss, Msw, Lcsw

* * *

I have known Jhiree since I was an intern. She has always maintained an inviting balance of professionalism and compassion. Her determination to overcome challenges is truly inspiring.

– LaToya Gaines, Psy.D.
NJ/NY Licensed Clinical Psychologist

* * *

Jhiree Davis-Jones, MEd, LPC will inspire you. An educator, a counselor, a compassionate human being, Jhiree is a mental health professional who believes in the quote "stay positive, work hard, make it happen." She knows all about shifting your life from powerless to empowered, investing in yourself, and self-care. Her enthusiasm and insight are unsurpassed - she will motivate you.

– Sharon Lynn Ryan MED, AABC
Social Media and Marketing Professional

* * *

Jhiree embodies a rare blend of intelligence, deep compassion, and personal strength. Having seen her growth professionally and personally throughout years has been nothing short of an honor. Jhiree stops at nothing to achieve the goals she has set out for herself in spite of the adversary she faces.

– Jose Luis Posos, M.Ed., LPC

* * *

I am proud to have known Jhiree for several years as a colleague and friend. She is an extraordinary empathic individual and therapist. Her qualities of bringing people together and creating mutual learning experiences related to our current world needs are more than exceptional.

– Dr. Kenneth Silvestri
Family, Couple, and Individual Psychotherapy
Certified Classical Homeopath

My *Current* PAST

FROM PAIN TO PURPOSE

An Empowering Story of
A Search for Love and My Mother's Addiction

My Current Past

From Pain to Purpose – An Empowering Story of A Search For
Love and My Mother's Addiction

Copyright © 2020 by **Jhiree Davis-Jones, M.Ed., LPC, NCC**

All rights reserved. Without prior written permission from the publisher, no part of this publication may be reproduced, stored in a retrievable system, or transmitted, in any form or by any means electronic, mechanical, photocopying, recording, or otherwise, except by the inclusion of brief quotations in review.

This book is a memoir. It reflects the author's present recollections of experiences over time. Some names and characteristics have been changed, some events have been compressed, and some dialogue has been recreated.

Published by: CHERRY BLOSSOM HEALING

– – – **www.AuthorJhiree.com** – – –

ISBN-13: 978-1-7348149-0-3

Category: Addiction, Memoir, Abandonment

Written by: Jhiree Davis-Jones | MyCurrentPast@gmail.com

Hair Stylist/MUA | Selena Smalls | @Lavishbylena

Cover Design & Book Formatted by: Eli Blyden Sr. | www.EliTheBookGuy.com

Printed in the USA by: A&A Printing & Publishing | www.PrintShopCentral.com

Dedication

To all my readers whose lives have been impacted
by an addiction – you are not alone.
May this book serve as a hug you've longed for,
a voice of reasoning, your support, a guide,
a book club discussion, and an inspiration for you to
begin your healing journey.

To my two beautiful red birds, Grandma Cherry and
Aunt Corstella, I will forever carry you both in my heart
and share a piece of you with every business venture.

Table of Contents

PART 3

My Current Past

Preface

This book will empower you to secure healthy boundaries with a loved one who is struggling with an addiction and place a greater value on your life without guilt.

As you travel along with me through journal entries and memories, you will learn ways to release emotions and share frustrations and insights as pathways to discovering a deeper understanding and healing through your past and present experiences.

Come with me to explore ways to overcome traumatic experiences and share discoveries that led me to my professional passion as a Licensed Professional Counselor (LPC).

Expect to be inspired about ways you too can take back your life!

My Current Past

Action

Pretend, pretend, I can't let anyone see
This terror called addiction is affecting me
Cameras rolling...

Sit up straight

Remember to speak properly

They're all watching you
Waiting to see if you'll do anything to resemble what she'd do
Be extremely productive
get degree after degree

so all can see there's just no stopping me.
Chin up, name brands, walk tall, dress well,
don't trip or they'll laugh, can't wait to see you fail
Hurry, your lipstick is almost gone, quickly reapply
before they start to question why
Be ready to defend yourself and how you ended up "odd,"
make perfect eye contact, and when uncertain, just smile
and nod

Perspiration, heart palpitating, palms are sweating,
adrenaline rushing,
my insides are busting
Can't let them see me panic
Slow strides,
catch my breath,
looking like a million bucks
as I fan it!
& CUT...

Whew, this damn girdle was blocking my air,
let me take this hot wig off, this ain't really my hair.
Wipe off this makeup 'cause I hate it
expensive shoes only to get congratulated
These lashes are falling

Wait where's the other one, can't recall it
Excuse me . . . What did you just say?

Cameras are still rolling?
Forget it, "Hi, it's the real me."
Now it's time to test my fate
and rescue my sanity!

My *Current* PAST

FROM PAIN TO PURPOSE

An Empowering Story of
A Search for Love and My Mother's Addiction

BY *Jhiree Davis-Jones*
M.Ed., LPC, NCC

My Current Past

Introduction

*M*y *Current Past* is a book inspired by my mother's drug addiction to crack cocaine and the detrimental influence it had on my life, from childhood to today. It is part of my journey in searching for ways to cope with my constant worries about my mom. I worried even during her periods of sobriety, fearing she would relapse. I realized that while she became addicted to the drug, I became addicted to curing her addiction.

Through my heartbreak, loss of hope, and desperate times of kneeling in the dark, asking God for help and answers, I have searched for ways to separate past influences from my current life—my current self. Through writing this book, I have found some of those answers and wish to share my discoveries with others who may be suffering in the same way.

Addiction not only impacts the user; it strongly affects the entire family. Traditions are broken. Holidays destroyed. It is a torture that sucks in the people closest to the addict and takes them on an unwanted journey of love, hate, detox, and disappointments. Your loved one fades away into someone who is unrecognizable, and you desperately yearn to awaken the loving person that he or she once was.

The vicious cycle of high hopes followed by disappointments haunted me throughout my life. Prior to journaling and throughout the process of creating this book, I struggled with the concept of my past and how I never felt like it belonged to me. Further though, and even more disturbing, was that my present did not feel like it belonged to me either. I felt both cheated and defeated. Why did I allow my mother's addiction to consume my past? And why does it continue to influence my present?

One worry that never left me was that, one day, someone would find my mom's lifeless, decomposed body. I lived in torment, anticipating that terrible phone call. And although I've grown in so many areas of my life, I am still haunted by this dreadful thought. The fact that I couldn't shake it left me disappointed in myself and feeling that, by now, I should have figured out how to keep her addiction from affecting my world.

From the outside in, I was very intelligent, professional, determined, successful, and well-put together. However, from the inside out, I was torn apart—a motherless child wishing for the day that I could visit my mom at her home, rather than at an abandoned building . . . dreaming of meeting my mother for tea or watching her play with my children, her grandchildren.

No one knew the struggle behind my brave front.

I eagerly shared with my mom that I was writing this book, secretly hoping it would be an inspiration to her. I thought maybe, just maybe, she would be interested in proving to the world that she could beat the addiction. However, I had to admit that this hope was just another attempt to try to save her.

I have accomplished much personally and professionally, but I've struggled to accept the rewards of those accomplishments. It all meant nothing, because to me, success equated to my mom's sobriety, which needed to be my greatest accomplishment.

Beyond revealing my hollow hopes, writing this book rescued my mental state. It gave me the opportunity to process the toll my mom's addiction had taken on my life. It became my safe space and an outlet to share my insecurities, anger, hurt, love, and disappointments surrounding her addiction. This book also became a reflection piece—a log, so to speak, of my efforts of trying to make my mom sober.

Today, I realize that my "little secret" about my mom's addiction, which I held onto throughout my life, and the pain experienced as a result, gave me an abundance of inner strength. These experiences made me unique and enabled me to see just how much I could bear without breaking. It was through this pain that I discovered my passion and my purpose.

After exhaustion and defeat settled in, and by the conclusion of this book, I was finally able to learn and accept that this battle was not mine. It was my mom's.

And now, I share my story in hopes of saving others who may be experiencing hopelessness and heartache from a loved one with an addiction. May you find peace in your efforts and be confident in understanding the reality that you did not cause the addiction; therefore, it is not your responsibility to cure it.

I love my mom with all my heart and wish only the best for her; however, I must follow my own path now, since I am responsible for the seeds I have planted in my own children. And every day, I must strive to be the mother to them that I have been chasing and longing for my entire life.

GUILTY

Some nights I feel guilty comfortably lying in my bed,
my feathered stuffed pillows softly resting beneath my head.

My body sinking into my memory foam
And slowly I sink into a memory or thought of my own.

I worry where my mom is resting.

Anxiety embraces, heart races, fears manifesting.

I picture her lying in an abandoned building,
dark alley or stairwell,
drowning in tears,
reflecting on her past,
and questioning how she ended up here.

Or could she be lying in bed next to a Mister with no name,
all to keep dry from the pouring rain.

Finally, I close my eyes to escape the pain.

Dear God, am I to blame?

Because the year I was born,
so was crack cocaine.

My mom is gone.

I am left alone with this shell of her being.

I fantasize about the day it will regain its life.

I'm sure she could teach me how to be an amazing woman
and wife.

I yearn for much advice on life
but I'm left without
and the scars resemble those of a knife.

How could one person cause so much pain?

My feelings race through stages of anger, hope, exhaustion,
and rage.

Finally, I'm back at square one . . .

I accept this as my life.

I give up.

Wipe my tears.

Hide my fears.

Journal these years.

And . . . just turn the DAMN page!

PART 1

Cherry

By My *Self*: trauma arises and lands me in the arms of an angel

THE START

"Jhiree, Jhiree, get up; let's go! We're going to your grandma's house. Come on, wake up! Hurry!" My dad's voice was demanding and would mark the first of several nights, which then turned into months and years of my sisters and me being separated. It was as if our paths were split in that very moment. My three older sisters were taken away and I ended up staying with my father's mother. My sisters all had the same father and I was the only child that my mother and father shared. Going to my grandmother's house alone was the first time that I was able to physically see and feel this divide. I was like a fish out of water! They were the peanut butter to my jelly!

Why did my dad break me away? Wait, where was my mom?

Prior to that moment, I hadn't seen her in about five days, which felt like an eternity.

Normally, she'd come back home about every other day. But not this time! Daddy became more and more worried one day after the next. I wanted her to come back to the house with us. When she'd go missing this way, our nightly routine was ruined. Since I was the baby, she'd place me on her lap and rock me to sleep while she and my sissies sang songs. While left at grandma's house, our favorite song repeated in my mind, "We are-we are, Climbing-climbing, Jacooobs ladder-ladder." She would take the lead and we were her backup singers. Now, here I stood alone, as a soloist.

I yearned to be with my sisters. We had gone through so much together and made it out together. The night we threw bleach on my dad to separate his and my mom's fight, we were a team! We made sure that we were safe, no matter what. Who would protect me now?

So many questions. But at five years old, no one's willing to answer. Well, honestly, that is. And I only had my experiences so far to try to sort through.

When we were back home, in Paterson, New Jersey, my mom would always disappear. At times, my sisters and I were so distracted that we didn't notice how long she was away. In the interim, my dad took care of us. Though he loved my mom, at times he seemed angry at her for being away from home so frequently. Once she'd return, they would argue. I guess he thought that if he moved her away from New Jersey, she would regain focus; it would be an opportunity for a fresh start. This escape was an attempt to save our family, and more importantly, her life.

So, we packed his red, two-door, Toyota Celica and headed south down Interstate 95. My mom and dad were in the front and my three sisters and I were behind them. It was pretty tight in the backseat, but we made the best of it. We sang "Don't Worry. Be Happy," by Bobby McFerrin, until, one at a time, we nodded off.

Sleepy Hollow Trailer Parks in Fayetteville, North Carolina was supposed to be the start of our new life! So, why am I now at my grandma's house? I wanted to hug my mommy really tight and beg her to stay home with us more. I knew that this would save our family. But, where was she?

Years later, I would learn that my dad left me in the arms of an Angel! So pure, God gave her a simple name, *Cherry*.

ABANDONED

At eight years old, I recall feeling like I was an abandoned child. At times I'd get angry and ask, "Grandma, when will I go back with my mom?"

Grandma would always respond with a calm voice, saying, "Jhiree, your momma has issues and cannot take care of you right now."

I whispered quietly enough so that only I could hear, "Why couldn't I go with Daddy, then?" I knew not to say it much louder as it would have hurt her feelings.

Daddy had been back in New Jersey for a little more than two years and it seemed that he was doing great. He visited me quite often and provided financial support for me to live with Grandma. This was great but, I wondered why I couldn't move back to Jersey to live with him. Finally, I decided that I would ask him the next time we spoke by phone.

"Daddy, can I come up there to live with you and everyone else?"

He replied, "The school system where you are is much better, Jhiree. Trust me."

The school system? Really, who cares about a "school system"? I only heard "Jhiree, you're staying with your grandma, so stop asking." I hated it! I made it my business to ask every time we spoke from then on. I figured one day he'd crack and would allow me to move back with him.

I wanted so badly to have my siblings around like everyone else! I wanted my parents to be at my shows, report card nights, and step team competitions. I wanted them in the crowd cheering for me and acting crazy like all the other parents on award nights. I'd pray so hard that they would surprise me. Soon, all these events, which were meant to be celebrations, turned out to be constant reminders that I was abandoned.

Many times, I was embarrassed because my friends' parents were much younger than Grandma. They were a lot cooler, too! My grandma did "grandma" things. She carried change in a sock, turned everything off during a storm, greased my scalp daily, and believed any music outside of Christian music was called "the blues."

As I grew older, I learned that grandma had a method to her madness. She used the sock so that people waiting online behind her would get frustrated enough to just give her the change she needed. What a genius!

SIBLING VISITS

One day, while in kindergarten, I was sitting in the cafeteria of my school and was about to bite into one of my school lunch favs, a BBQ riblet sandwich, when an announcement interrupted me.

"Will Jhiree Davis please report to the main office?" the principal stated.

A bit annoyed, I placed the sandwich back on the plastic tray and I left the table. I looked at the floor because I figured it was never good news when someone was called to the principal's office. Once I arrived, the principal reached out her hand. I hesitantly grabbed it and held tight.

My palms were sweating as we walked out the main entrance. I grew anxious as I noticed that there was a navy-blue station wagon with the family services emblem on it, parked right in front of my school. This was the same symbol that was on all the cars at the visiting site where I'd go to see my sisters on Wednesdays. I examined the car further. My pupils dilated and filled with excitement. I noticed my sisters were in the back seat! All three of them!

"What are they doing here?" I whispered and wondered why this visit was being held at my school, and during school hours. Maybe they were taking us all out someplace special. I smiled, nervously. I mean, who was I fooling? Good things do not usually happen for us. Not as a unit. I always looked forward to our visits. Normally, they were held in a small room located in a huge building.

Suddenly, I realized my sisters hadn't gotten out of the car. This visit was strange. The car door didn't fly open as fast as it usually does. No one raced to hug me. My sisters got out, one by one, and looked about as if they were lost. I was flustered by what was happening. Looks of desperation and hopelessness invaded their faces. As they walked closer to me, I detected tears running down their cheeks. Finally, we embraced one another tightly. I began crying too because I could feel their sadness. They shared what was happening. We embraced even tighter, and our tears were accompanied by weeping voices filled with disappointment and heartbreak. I learned this would be the last time I'd see them for quite some time.

GRANDMA'S HOUSE

Growing up with Grandma made me feel like I was an only child. This was like a gift and a curse, simultaneously. I was able to raid the refrigerator without having to share and at the start of every month, I received fourteen dollars' worth of food stamps to buy ANYTHING I wanted! You couldn't tell me I wasn't rich! During this time of the month, I was on top of the world! I had lots of money—well, food stamps—and all the friends. My house was the most popular on the block.

My friends and I would gather on my porch and we'd pretend to have a picnic. We had the music turned up all the way and would sing and dance along.

Since I was the only child, I was able to watch whatever I wanted and do whatever I wanted. Life was great! Except, it really wasn't, because all those material things couldn't fill the void, I was feeling from being abandoned by my family. I felt like my sisters and mom had forgotten about me and I was by myself.

"Do this and do that!" These were the constant directives given by James.

"I'm tired, you need to try to do some things yourself," I'd say back to him.

"Stop being fresh, you crack baby!" he yelled.

Wait. What?? Did he just call me a crack baby?

My mom started drugs several years after I was born. How am I a crack baby? What does that even mean? Am I different than regular kids? These questions cycled through my brain and multiple answers surfaced. The more unpleasant the answers became, visuals accompanied them, and in my heart grew a burning sensation.

Tears ran down my cheeks as I went to find Grandma. I hurried from room to room. I needed to find her. I whispered to God, "Please, don't let this be true!" Finally, I found her outside in the backyard, humming gospel hymns and hanging laundry on the clothes lines.

"Girl, what's idling you?" she asked. I tried to share what James said but my lips trembled so much that the words weren't coming out correctly. Finally, she understood. But rather than answer, she hugged me tight and said, "Here. Here." As I leaned against her chest, I could hear her fast-paced heartbeat. She grew furious at my pain and dropped the wooden clothes pins into the basket at her feet. "Let's go!" she yelled and hurried in the house with me in tow. "James, why would you say something so stupid?"

"Shut up, *bitch*, before I hit you with my cane," James responded. You see, grandma's husband, James, had suffered a stroke and had to use a wheelchair and cane to get around. He could not bathe, get dressed, or transition from wheelchair to sofa without her help. However, this did not stop him from verbally—and at times, physically— abusing her.

If she were close enough to him during these heated arguments, he'd hit her with his cane. I remember thinking, "Wow! She was the perfect wife and catered to his every need. She cooked his meals. She made sure he always had *Black and Mild's* to smoke and SHE helped him get in and out of bed." Yet he still treated her like what I considered "trash."

These experiences taught me never to wait on a man hand and foot. I also learned that if you treat a man similarly to how Grandma treated James, he would interpret it as a weakness. Although I loved my grandma, I vowed to be the complete opposite of her when it came to marriage. This was supposed to be my safe haven, but more and more it reminded me of my experiences with my own parents. These paired experiences taught me early that marriage and relationships were full of pain and suffering.

* * *

PROFESSIONAL DISCOVERY

In my therapeutic experience, I learned that children who are exposed to volatile situations feel powerless. They become fearful and anxious in most settings. They are on guard and await the next fight or argument. They do not feel safe and worry what will trigger the next traumatic event. At times, they even feel that they are the cause of the dysfunction. Future relationships are heavily influenced by this exposure.

Grandma was a praying woman. She attended church nearly every week. As the preacher would give his sermon, she'd sit clutching her purse tightly on her lap while shaking her head. Her face seemed to show disdain toward the preacher's message. Yet she totally agreed with what he was saying. She lived life by the word of God. She'd sing gospel songs throughout the house. When she couldn't recall the words, she was not discouraged. She'd say "something and something another" to fill in the blank and would keep singing as if she'd mastered the lyrics. It was so hilarious!

At times she'd look back to see if I had noticed the missed words. If I did, we'd burst out laughing.

Continuous praise demonstrated how committed she was to her religion. On numerous occasions, I'd witness her shout her praises while running from one end of our small home to the other. On a daily basis it appeared as if she forgave James. Seems she did not hold grudges and would allow him a fresh start every morning.

She had faith that God was in control. "Jhiree, sometimes you pray to God and you ask him to fix things. Guess what, you may not always like how He fixes it. But He shaw will fix it! You see, James had that dere stroke. God had had enough!"

Grandma swore by her wedding vows, which she reminded me of quite often. "Until death do you part," she'd say quickly, while grinning. She was the sweetest, kindest, and most giving person I knew. It hurt to see her treated that way by James, and at times, it left me angry. Oddly, I admired the value she placed on marriage.

I felt helpless when they would have those huge fights. I felt even more helpless when I'd have fights. These feelings were magnified every time I was involved in fights and arguments at school or in the neighborhood. I hated knowing that I had siblings but had to live as an "only child" with my grandma. I wished my sisters were there to have my back. When in conflict, I could hear their voices in my head. My oldest sister would say, "Who's bothering my 'lil sister?" If the answer wasn't what she wanted, she was always willing and prepared to fight! Then, my second to the oldest sister would not say anything at ALL, because she spoke super-fast and stuttered. She feared she would not be understood. So, she'd just start fighting and ask questions later. Lastly, but not the least of my opponent's worries, was my sister next to me. My mom called her "the knee baby." She'd be a little more patient. She'd wait for the opponent to try to explain what the problem was. She wouldn't threaten much. The look in her eyes and her tone let others know that she was not to be taken lightly.

Yup, that was my team! When we were together, everyone knew not to come near this "little sister." However, when apart, I was left with only their voices in my head and had to battle each encounter alone.

From here, the rest of my life would be spent repaying my sisters for our separation. Years upon years, I felt like I was treated better and given a more solid foundation. For this, I'd live in guilt and go the extra mile to make sure my sisters were okay. Sometimes that meant lending or giving money, rides here and there, taking them to dinner, or a spa. I'd fall back on arguments, because I believed that would just add fuel to their traumatic pasts.

From what they shared with me, once they left the school that day, they had gone to several foster homes and finally ended up back in New Jersey. I could only imagine the devastation they incurred. Yet a piece of me envied the fact that they were together.

PROFESSIONAL DISCOVERY

In families of separated children, siblings' relationships become important. They rely heavily on one another to provide support and nurture what would normally be fulfilled by the absent parent.

In some cases, separation into foster care and/or infrequent visits can potentially damage sibling relationships. Unfortunately, in most cases, many of these relationships either weaken or disintegrate. Ultimately, this could lead to permanent estrangement; thus, breaking the sibling bond which was once strong.

Attempts to reunite or mend these relationships may be unsuccessful, and resentment and hatred may prevail. It is difficult to identify the absent parent as the sole blame. Rather, some measure is bestowed among the siblings. Siblings in such situations are left to mourn the loss of their relationships or constantly struggle to repair. Family therapy is highly recommended.

JERSEY SUMMERS

"Mrs. Cherry, I've been clean now for two years. Can Jhiree come to Jersey to spend the summers with us?" My mom had been clean and stable for an entire two years and my dad and grandma agreed to allow me to spend the summers in Jersey. At this time, both my parents had mates and I would split time between both houses.

Every year toward the last day of school, I'd become more and more anxious. A very small piece of me was sad to leave my grandma alone, but a huge piece desired to be reunited with my mom, dad, and sisters.

In school, I was pretty popular because I was "going up north." Grandma called it "up the road." Everything cool—trends, food, and accents—came from "up north." My classmates would ask me to speak funny like the people from up north. I'd go with the flow and say a sentence that added w's and r's in words where, in the south, they didn't belong. "Put your coWffee and sauWsage next to the hot doWg," I'd say. At times my friends would mimic the accent, too. They'd say silly things like, "Oh my goWd, you going to bring back some waRter!" It was hilarious! We'd always burst out laughing because we knew just how ridiculous we sounded! On the contrary, once I arrived in the North, they'd tease me about my southern accent. They'd say I spoke so "country." But I didn't mind one bit because within a week I'd always pick up their accent. I'd slip back into the southern from time to time, but for the most part, I did not let them catch me.

Summer visits were the start of rebuilding and reconnecting with my mom and sisters. I was the youngest, so everyone spoiled me. I was also the only child when I'd go to my dad's. I pretty much got what I wanted with him as well. It was the best of both worlds.

Since my birthday was in the summer, my mom always planned a house party. We'd go shopping for party favors, games, and decorations, all around downtown Paterson. I was the happiest kid on earth. It was as if my parents and siblings were making up for lost time.

One summer, my mom got me a gold ring for almost every finger. Things were great and we picked up right where we had left off.

Though I was almost as big as she was, my mom would still put me on her lap. She and my three older sisters would rock back and forth, singing those same songs which required us to follow her lead. It was our unique thing and we loved it! It was just like old times!

During the weeknights and on some weekends, my sisters and I would attend Narcotics Anonymous (NA) meetings with my mom and stepdad. My mom would find someone new at every meeting to introduce me to. She'd smile ear to ear while bouncing anxiously in her seat, filled with excitement. "This is my baby that I was telling you about that lives down south," she'd say. The introductions didn't stop there! She'd proudly introduce me to all her friends that we'd bump into around the town as well.

Some days, my dad would pick me up from my mom's and we'd hang out in New York City, go to carnivals, take road trips, or go to amusement parks. You name it and he was giving me, his only child, the experience! During these summer visits, I started to notice that his girlfriend wasn't too fond of how he treated me. She would give me awkward stares and would tell on me almost every time I thought I was getting away with something. I wanted so badly for her to be a "cool" stepmom, but I could tell that she had no desire.

RETURN TO SENDER

I never looked forward to returning home. We started school earlier than Jersey. It was not fair that I always had to miss out on the rest of the summer fun.

Upon my return, Grandma would run to the door with a huge grin on her face! She'd squeeze me for dear life and pat my back as hard as a determined and aggressive parent trying to get their baby to burp. This was always paired with her unbearable and obnoxious laugh "Ahh ha ha haaaa." she'd say. "My fourth child is home!"

I never accepted the idea of being her "fourth" child. In fact, I despised the title because I was my mom's fourth child. If I was Grandma's fourth that would mean I did not have a mom. I never understood why she would say this. Didn't she know it hurt my feelings? Maybe she thought I needed to feel a sense of belonging, or maybe she wanted me to feel like I had a "full-time" mother. Although I didn't; I loved my mom and always knew we'd be reunited. I dreamed of the day we'd all live together again. I yearned for what I once had and believed that, one day, God would answer my prayers.

When people would ask my grandma how many children she had, she'd always say four. I showed disdain in my facial expressions, though she couldn't see most of the times. The more she'd say it, the closer I grew to disclosing my true feelings of the inference. While I knew she had positive intentions, I also felt it diminished what my real mom and I were trying to rebuild.

When I finally found the nerve to tell my grandma, I realized immediately after that it didn't come out like I had planned.

"Grandma, would you *stop* calling me your child; you are not my mother!" I pleaded. The look on her face was that of distress and at that very moment I regretted my words.

I should have given a second thought and considered her feelings a bit more. My delivery was completely wrong. But it was out, and I could not take those hurtful words back.

There I sat, feeling like a monster, as she stared at me in a loss for words. She looked down as if she was disappointed. Though I wished my approach had been a bit more subtle, I was relieved that I had finally let her in on how the title made me feel. I wanted her to understand that I loved her, but as my grandma. She needed to know that although I had a short time with my mom, she was still my mom and I did not want to replace her.

There's just something special about my mommy that was impossible for anyone to duplicate. Our unique bond, paired with life's experiences, deeply connected us. These experiences started at conception and would continue for a lifetime, no matter what. I loved her to death and didn't want people to talk badly about her absence.

Yes, my mom made many mistakes; however, I was certain that as soon as she realized one of those mistakes was leaving me behind, she would, without a doubt, come for me.

I played out this day over and over in my mind. When my mom was ready, I wanted everyone to greet her with open arms. I dreamed about the day this would happen and how I'd finally get to experience what happy tears felt like.

Summer visits continued for about three years. The returns to the south became more and more agonizing. Once I completed seventh grade, I asked my grandma if I could go live in NJ with my mom and dad. "Can I please, please stay in Jersey for just my eighth-grade year? Please!" I begged, with my "sad face" and nagging voice. "They have a prom and a graduation up there, and we don't!" I added.

I told her I'd go for just one year. I promised to move back with her after.

At this point, James's health had declined. He resided in a rest home. My aunt, who once lived with us, went away to college in Ohio. We were the only two left in the house.

Grandma did not respond to the question. She stood emotionless and numb. I didn't know if I should have hugged her or run away. She looked as if I had sucked the life out of her. The light I once brought to her eyes was turned off. She didn't say a word—just slowly walked away and lay down on her bed. It was a pretty quiet night.

The next morning, she selflessly said, "Jhiree, I reckon you can go. I know you're not coming back, but I'll be okay . . ."

PROFESSIONAL DISCOVERY

Many times, abandoned children crave additional love, not "replaced" love. Children need constant reassurance. They yearn for validation, commitment and to belong. Though uncomfortable, discuss the "elephant in the room", which is their missing parent(s). Assure them that you are willing to answer any questions they may have when they are ready. Offer unwarranted hugs and affirmations. Understand that there is a void that is present at times, no matter how much you've attempted to overcompensate. This approach will allow them to embrace and appreciate your unconditional compassion. As they mature, they will be forever grateful for your role and impact on their life. They'll have a greater understanding of your sacrifices and commitment to their well-being. Great job!

My Current Past

PART 2

Blossom

Self-Discovery: a search for answers, reconnection, and hope

REUNITED

My dream came true! I was once again a resident of Paterson, NJ! There I was on cloud nine and reunited with my mom, dad, and sisters! My mom registered me for eighth grade right away. I was getting settled in this summer, rather than just visiting. I was in utter disbelief! My life had never gone this right. Me?! Living in the same home again with my mom and sisters. I was even in walking distance of my dad's.

"What!?" I recall, saying aloud. "Go me, go me!" as I broke out into my happy dance!

Yet sometimes, when no one was watching, I'd cry. I'd cry for two separate reasons at the same time.

The first was that I could not stop thinking about how lonely my grandma must be. I felt guilty for leaving her there all alone. Who'd read the small print for her now? Who'd help her sort through her unorganized phone contact book? Who'd help her remember where she had parked her car? Who would she offer snacks to in the middle of the night?

The second was that I was elated to be a part of my original family unit again! I looked forward to having sibling tiffs and couldn't wait for the opportunity to have my sisters stand up for me like old times. My mom and I would make eye contact and I knew she was just as happy as I was that her baby was now with her forever! I felt like

I was watching a surprise episode of a discontinued favorite television show. We were overjoyed!

Crying for the both at the same time led to lots of confusion. I'd dry my tears quickly, so they weren't questioned and continued soaking in my new reality, because this was where I belonged!

Approximately one month after I settled in NJ, I received a call from my dad. "Your grandma had a heart attack!", he said.

I could not believe what I heard. "What did I do?" I said. "I should have been there!" Tears poured profusely from my eyes. With blurred vision, I choked and couldn't utter another word. My throat hurt as if someone was tightly squeezing it. I clutched my stomach to grasp the pain. I was torn. Should I have stayed with my mom, dad, and siblings or should I have gone back to take care of the one person who had taken care of me?

The pain from my throat and stomach traveled to my chest. I wanted to be there for her. I needed to let my grandma know that I still loved her even though we were apart. I wanted to give her a hug and say sorry for causing her that much heartache.

"How could I abandon the very person who took me in as her own?"

I wanted to hear her laugh obnoxiously and stomp the floor, disturbing all neighbors. I wanted my grandma back! The more I thought of her, the more empathetic and powerless I felt. But my dad thought it best I stay behind. He said that my going and leaving her once again would probably make matters worse. This only confirmed what I already knew.

"I caused grandma's heart attack!" Everyone, including me, thought this heart attack was my fault. I only needed to hear her voice for her to convince me I was wrong.

At this moment of feeling helpless and alone, it hit me. "What if Grandma dies?" My voice echoed as I spoke into my clasped hands. I needed to pray!

Grandma had a very close relationship with God. She'd say, "Jhiree, remember to always pray, and see don't God answer ya! See, He may not come when you want him, but He's right on time."

So, I prayed. "Dear Lord, please allow my grandma to pull through. I miss her so much! I just want to see her again. Also, if you ever decide to take her from me, please prepare me, God. Please! I can't imagine my life without her. She's my best friend, my second mom, my foundation. Father, God, don't take her now. I'm not ready. PLEASE!"

I wasn't too good at praying, but I knew just what I wanted to say. Grandma said he'd answer. She never lied, so I had faith He wouldn't disappoint. I now regretted my decision to leave her.

I understood my dad's reasoning for leaving me behind, but my heart was not as accepting. I later learned that my grandma had a mild heart attack. After only one month of recovery, things were back to normal.

Once I finally spoke with her, I was relieved to learn that she did not blame me for the heart attack. She continued to love me as her own. God had answered my prayer! It was then that I established my own relationship with Him. I no longer had to send prayers through Grandma. This experience was proof that I was now old enough for Him to hear me directly.

KNIGHT-TIME

My first day of John F. Kennedy high school was a bit embarrassing, to say the least. I had come to Paterson the summer prior to eighth grade. Seven months into the school year, I was required to sit for their standardized state assessments. The other students had been preparing for several years, and here I sat, brand new! As expected, I completely bummed it! I later learned that my performance on that test would determine my path for high school.

As I sat in the auditorium, anxious and uncertain of what was ahead, I was confident about one thing, I looked "super fresh." I had on new everything! I smiled proudly at my ensemble several times. My view was interrupted as the teacher stood over me and handed me a schedule.

"Jhiree Davis?" she asked to make sure.

"Yes, thank you," I replied as I reached for the schedule.

The words REMEDIAL MATH stood out like a sore thumb. My esteem was immediately crushed, and I began to lower myself in my seat. My outer body immediately aligned with my inner emotions. I was so embarrassed I wanted to disappear. A little piece of me knew that they had misjudged me. I would spend my freshman year proving that they had made a huge mistake.

As days turned into months that little piece of certainty grew. Midway through my freshman year, after receiving all high grades in math and the rest of my subjects, I was offered to be in STEM (a program for the "smart" students). I thought to myself, *This path is pretty easy, why should I go over there to possibly struggle?* I quickly rejected the offer and continued school as a "normal" student. Things were going so well that I decided to try out for the marching band's dance team. They were called the Nasty Knights. Although my dad despised the name, I made it! I was excited to see what my journey as a Nasty Knight would entail!

Freshman year was a breeze. I met many new friends, but for some reason established a great connection with my male peers. By the close of freshmen year, they outnumbered my female friends.

During that summer one of my closest male friends introduced me to his best friend. "Jhiree, I want you to meet Corey," he said as he smiled. I could tell he was up to something. His friend was super attractive, and I quickly looked down so as not to make any more eye contact. He was the type that Grandma said she liked. He had a nice build with muscles, *Check!* He was light-skinned, *Check*! And he was tall, *Check*!

I wanted to make sure that my eyes weren't fooling me, so I peeked at him once more. This time, I was mesmerized! My eyes would not allow me to look down again. My palms started to sweat, and I grinned from ear to ear. I smiled so much it felt as if my cheeks had been lifting weights. Finally, words left my lips as I stuck out my hand and prepared for a firm handshake.

With constant eye contact, I said, "Hello, nice to meet you Corey." I was proud of myself because I kept it very professional. However, this did not satisfy my friend.

"Really Jhiree, a handshake? Come on, you can do better. Give him a hug!" he said.

Nervously, I opened my arms and reluctantly prepared for a hug. Strangely, I found myself patting him on his back, sort of like how my grandma always patted me.

Once I reached home, I could not get him off my mind. He was F-ine! He was taller and older than me. More importantly, he was respectful! But I was not allowed to have boyfriends, so if anything came of this he'd be "a boy . . . that was my friend."

Many days of my summer were spent daydreaming about the moment we met.

On the second day of school in my sophomore year, I heard a male voice say, "Jhiree, you never used that number." I looked over and *oh-my-gosh*, it was him!

Finally, my life seemed "normal" and things were on track. My mom was doing great! She faithfully attended Narcotics Anonymous (NA) meetings with her husband, who was also in recovery. They were on a mission to beat their addictions. They were committed and followed the twelve steps of the program to a "T".

I was proud of my mom and stepfather's dedication to their sobriety. NA had become the prevalent focus of our lives. To us, it was the glue that held our family together. Therefore, we wanted it just as badly as they did. Maybe even more. We attended meetings with them three to four times per week. My mom and stepfather readily became sponsors. They spent countless hours encouraging others to stay on track at their most tempting moments.

When my mom or stepfather shared in the group, we would all stop what we were doing and listen attentively. This was where I learned of their true struggles with their addictions. At times, they shared their thoughts about relapsing and how their commitment to NA helped them prevent it. This made me nervous. I would get butterflies in my stomach. I hated the thought of my family being torn apart once again due to crack cocaine.

At the close of every meeting, my sisters and I would join the group. We looked forward to chanting the mantra along with the recovering addicts in attendance. The entire group would stand up and form a circle. They would wrap their arms behind the person next to them to close the circle. My sisters and I squeezed in wherever we would or wouldn't fit and followed the lead of the adults. Once we made eye contact with one another, we'd giggle. Finally, we'd yell along with the group, "Keep coming back! It works when you work it! So, work it and live!"

U-TURN

A t the conclusion of my sophomore year, my mom and stepdad decided they wanted to have a child of their own. My mom constantly shared how badly she wanted a boy. She decided to test her fate and had her tubes untied. Months later, to everyone's surprise, we learned that not only was she pregnant, but she was actually having a baby BOY! Shortly after, I learned that my dad's mate was also expecting a baby boy!

I was happy and distraught. I had been my mom's baby and my dad's only child for sixteen years. Now that I was back, I did not mind keeping this spot forever! I was not ready to give it up! However, I was far too involved in high school to dwell.

Shortly after giving birth to my baby brother, my mom would go missing for hours at a time. She gained new friends and spent endless hours at the "store." Next, we noticed she was openly smoking cigarettes. Then, she'd drink beer. Finally, she needed her cigarettes with her beer, and soon after would finish this pattern with a trip to the "store."

We grew concerned with those store visits when she'd return home empty handed and unable to make eye contact. My mom started to avoid the NA life all together. She refused to attend meetings with my stepdad so he would go alone. We knew she was slipping, but no one wanted to accept that she had relapsed.

After nearly six years of sobriety, I was devastated. I thought, *How could she be so selfish? How could she do this to my little brother? Why would she make him suffer the way we did?*

The more she became submerged in the addiction, the more I became committed to parenting my baby brother. He relied on me for consistent nurturing. My heart broke for him! I wanted to protect him from all the negative things that my sisters and I had been exposed to due to her addiction. But what exactly could I offer a one year old, when I was just a kid myself?

School had become a positive distraction.

PROFESSIONAL DISCOVERY

In my experience, I have learned that with children of parents suffering with addictions, expectations are unclear and the parent's role is inconsistent and at times, nonexistent. The lack of structure often means that children are left to take on greater self-reliance. They may or may not gain confirmation from the parent regarding their own insecurities. In addition to the parent being absent for their social emotional well-being, the parent is also absent from their household responsibilities. Children may be responsible for maintaining the responsibilities of the home. At times the parent/child roles are reversed. This burden becomes too much for their cognitive abilities.

FOCUSED

Ligh school allowed me the opportunity to create my own identity. One aside from my mom's flaws. It was a place where her choices no longer made me feel "unworthy." I planned to keep her addiction a "secret" from my peers. I'd also purposely not tell Grandma about my mom's relapse, because she'd request I return to North Carolina. And there was no way I was leaving my little brother behind!

I was so disappointed in my mom's choices. What about all those NA meetings she, well . . . WE attended? What about the people she sponsored and who looked up to her for hope? What about "our" serenity prayer that was supposed to bring her strength? My sisters and I learned that thing by heart and we proudly said it alongside of her at every meeting. "God grant me the serenity to accept the things I cannot change, the courage to change the things I can, and the wisdom to know the difference," we'd say in harmony. We felt unified! Like nothing could ever break us up again.

"All of that was for what?" I questioned, full of animosity. I grew angry and frustrated. Many nights I cuddled with my baby brother and cried myself to sleep. My childhood had come back to haunt me. I feared just how bad things would get this time around. My anger would dissolve quickly and would turn into sadness. I prayed she'd make it out alive this time.

Helplessness prevailed and I found myself once again trapped in the body of that five-year-old little girl. I still had so many questions. I relied on the handful of people who I had shared the relapse with at school and home for support. I found myself just as afraid as in the past. I felt abandoned and disheveled at times, but I refused to be powerless. Thankfully, my external façade masked the internal occurrences.

When I was overwhelmed and could no longer face the addiction alone, I shared how it had impacted my life with a small group of peers in *The Teen Center* at school. This place had become my safe space and home away from home. We played games, ate dinner, and discussed areas of weaknesses which directly affected our lives. We felt comfortable to disclose our deepest, darkest insecurities and heartaches. Our discussions ranged from deaths in our families to STDs. There was no topic too taboo to touch. All the staff was invested in our well-being and would extend themselves unselfishly. I looked forward to attending the after-school services at least three to four times weekly.

During my junior year, I was cast as Myrtle Mae in the school play, *Harvey*. This was a blessing in disguise. This main role served as a healthy distraction from my chaotic home.

Late-night rehearsals meant I had very little time to worry about my mom and her addiction. This was paired with dancing in the marching band—when in season—and hanging at *The Teen Center* after school. Yet I must admit I did worry about my little brother nonstop. I would find a little peace knowing that my stepfather was very much present for him. This enabled me to continue being a kid on many days.

The play turned out to be a huge success! And although we had several shows, I can't recall if Mommy ever made it to one. She had stopped doing anything productive once she reunited with crack.

At the conclusion of my junior year, to my surprise, I was crowned during our Camelot celebration as Miss Drama Queen. I was told that this was due to my dedication to the production. Ironically, I was crowned Miss Life Management as well.

I recall thinking, "Hmmm. Drama Queen and Miss Life Management, my life exactly." Somehow, through all the disappointments, I still managed to stay focused.

"Jhiree, keep the sun in your face to see where you're going and the wind at your back to help get you there." and "Good-better-best, never let it rest until the good gets better and the better gets best!" These were my dad's favorite quotes. On my most challenging days, his words of wisdom would repeat in my mind. He always knew exactly what to say when I was discouraged and needed a boost. Rather than using my life experiences as a handicap and playing victim, I channeled all of the anger into positive ways to enhance my academics.

During this year, I was also selected to be the mistress of ceremony for my school's major events. I recall being both nervous and excited to speak, all at once. I disliked my voice and was afraid I'd pronounce people's last names incorrectly. After the first event, I quickly lost this fear and grew to understand and appreciate how much of a privilege it was to be selected. I recall my dad's girlfriend saying to me, after attending one of these events, "You make me feel like a celebrity. Everyone has such nice things to say about you!" I smiled at this statement, but still wondered why she never really liked me. Anyway, this was huge because I presented awards to all sorts of important people throughout our district and community. Yet, my mom's absence reminded me of how she had missed all of my events in the past.

One day, as I entered the school, I saw a flyer that read: *Paterson Teachers for Tomorrow (PT4T). If you're interested in receiving a full scholarship to become a teacher, please come out to our meeting to find out more!* I stopped in my tracks, as if the sign was a commercial that I was watching. As I came to, I realized my cheeks were on fire from smiling all that time. I walked to homeroom, dazed about someday becoming a teacher and having my very own classroom!

During the first meeting, I met representatives from William Paterson University (WPU) who shared details about steps needed to qualify for their scholarship. There were a few high school teachers present and maybe about eight other interested students. I learned that we had to attend two meetings per month and maintain a 3.0 GPA in order to be accepted. I felt confident! My grades were great, and I had no problem committing to the meetings. Then they finally mentioned that only three students could be selected from the three major high schools in our town. *Dammit*, I thought. Learning this was a bit discouraging, but memories of conquering freshman year surfaced, and I was up for the challenge.

Though my junior year at school was awesome, my home life was devastating. Some nights I'd get home and would have to find dinner. My mom's hours of being missing had turned into days just like when we were in NC. Many nights I taught my baby brother his alphabet and colors while I gave him a bath. I prayed that his dad and I had taken care of him so well that he didn't notice my mom's absence.

I learned to love him as if I was his mother.

At times, I looked into his precious big, bright eyes and I'd see myself at five years old! As I struggled to untangle my experiences from his, my nose tingled with a burning sensation. Tears rolled down my face. I did not want him to go through any of what my sisters and I had gone through.

"Hadn't she had enough?" I constantly questioned why she went through with having her tubes untied, just to have a boy if she was not going to enjoy him. I'd quickly wipe away my tears so he would not see me crying. Someone had to be strong for him.

Quite often, Mom would come back into the house to change clothes several times throughout the day. When asked why, she'd say, "Girl, be quiet. I don't want people to know what I had on." On other occasions, she would come inside the house and start searching everywhere. She'd destroy the entire house! She moved furniture, took out clothes from hampers, threw pillows on the floor, and felt in between the tight spaces of the sofa.

After a while, we'd ask what she was looking for. She would respond in a frantic voice, "I hid my shit from myself! I know it's here!" Once she realized just how silly she looked, she would start laughing. Her life had taken some devastating and familiar steps backwards. Rather than chasing us, her children, or at least her one-year-old son, she chased crack cocaine. Our roles had reversed and, sadly, I started to feel like I was raising her.

I was ashamed of her addiction. I constantly worried about what people would say if they found out. I feared they would judge or tease me because of her actions.

My mom had quickly hit her rock bottom. She would sell food from our refrigerator back to the stores. Anything that was of value to us, she knew would be of value to someone in the streets. It was all for sale!

Luckily, I didn't have to keep her away from school because she didn't seem interested in my academics. I purposely hid important dates and events from her. This included award ceremonies and huge accomplishments, just in case she decided to show up.

In my mom's absence at such a pivotal time, I had hoped I could turn to my dad's girlfriend for guidance and advice.

My dad loved her, and I wanted to love her, too! I quickly started to question her true feelings towards me, as I seemed to be the center of every argument or disagreement between her and my dad. The more my dad praised and spoiled me, the larger their fights grew. I tried to ignore all the signs of her disliking me because I wanted so badly to experience what it was like to have a "normal" mom. However, year after year, our relationship became unbearably strained.

By the time I reached my senior year of high school, I had gained many friends! People got me! Well, not the "home" me, but they embraced and accepted the "school" me. They laughed at my jokes, complimented my style, made me feel confident, and, more importantly, they trusted me. My peers grew to not only like me, but they respected me as well. It was as if they, too, saw how bright I was. They trusted me with secrets and asked me for advice. We even created silly names for one another. They believed in me— and when elections came around for senior class president, they encouraged me to run. To my surprise, I won!

At that moment, my life had changed for the better! I was in shock for the first two minutes after the announcement revealed that I had won. My peers did not know, but I immediately flashed back over my entire life! They had no idea what I had gone through and how much this opportunity truly meant to me. I felt like I belonged and they were my family! I was in awe! This was the first time that I released tears of joy.

I couldn't wait to share the news with everyone. And even decided that if I found my mom in a sober state, I'd share the news with her. Otherwise . . . I'd keep it to myself.

I called Grandma first. "A-Ha-Ha", she laughed loudly through the phone. "I prayed on it, girl, and I knew you'd do it! God-almighty-knows, I got a mind to shout!" I heard her fist pounding against the arm of her favorite spot on the sofa. Her heels beating up the floor as she stomped and laughed obnoxiously. She was excited for my accomplishment and was always my biggest fan. She was the loudest, most-dedicated cheerleader.

I prayed faithfully on a nightly basis and sometimes twice a night, "God, please, please, prepare me for the day she leaves me." I loved her more than life itself!

Next, I phoned my dad. "Way to go, you, in there!" he said. "They must've known your daddy was Big Daddy D!" he continued. I felt his grin through the phone. Then he went on to tell me, for the fifteenth time, about how he was President of off-campus students when he was in college and blah, blah, blah. Finally, he came back to me. "Congratulations once again on your success; I am proud of you, young lady!" This was just the balance I needed to keep me focused when my mind would revisit the nightmare of my mom's addiction.

My high school experience gave me the confirmation that I needed. The support I received empowered me to strive for any and every goal that I ever wanted. It provided the guidance I never received from my mother. Friends, teachers, and mentors gave me the hugs that I longed for from her. My attendance in school provided me the stability that I lacked from home. Academic accomplishments enabled me to receive tons of praise and acknowledgements from peers and staff that my mom neglected to give me. More importantly, school made me feel like I was someone special. I absolutely loved it! It was my peace in the midst of the many storms at home. I was liked and my life had way more in store. For these reasons, I knew that I would stay in school for as long as I possibly could.

My mom's addiction could not destroy ME!

As I was preparing for graduation, I learned that I was selected to receive the PT4T full scholarship! "YESSSS! College here I come!" I shouted! I'd be the first of my mother's children to attend college!

I had come to realize that I had a unique ability to connect with people, and although I wanted to be a teacher first, my passion was to continue touching people's lives. I knew that if I could successfully get out of this situation, I could help others to get through their issues as well.

I wanted to be a psychologist!

Throughout the toxic exposure to my mom's addiction, my "friend" Corey had been my shoulder to lean on. Although he never knew what it was like to have a parent battling with an addiction, he ensured that I did not miss out on the necessities. He tried his best to provide for me the things that my mom did not. Many times, this would mean meals, school shopping, and just being a listening ear. When I'd get out of school late, he'd be there so that I would not walk alone.

I finally got the nerve to officially introduce my "boyfriend" to my dad, three years after we were already dating. The smirk on my dad's face suggested that he was either pleased or disgusted.

When I lived in N.C., my dad talked about me to his students anytime an opportunity presented itself. He would even go so far as to pull out a photo of me. He allowed each student to come up to see it. One day, during his routine photo sharing, a student said, "Man, she's cute! I bet I can get your daughter if I wanna!"

My dad quickly replied, "Young man, please sit down. I highly doubt that. Besides, my daughter lives down south." As the student proceeded to his seat, he continued to tell his friends, "I bet I could get his daughter!"

My dad said he laughed at the student and continued to teach. Who would have known that seven years later I'd be standing before my dad, introducing this former student as my very first boyfriend? Nine years later, my dad shared this same story at our wedding reception. He now continues to share it with our three children. He and my husband laugh about it quite often. I guess we were destined to be!

COLORISM

Throughout life, I was constantly told that I was "pretty TO BE dark-skinned." Over time, I began to believe this because I heard it from many people in different settings.

As I grew older, I internalized their opinions. I concluded that the underlying message was that it was a known fact that "dark-skinned" people were "Ugly." Although I was a darker brown, when people made jokes, they referred to me as "black." I hated taking photos and needed to double check that the flash was on. I yearned for other dark-skinned people to prove how beautiful we were, but I didn't see anyone on the television or in magazines.

To me, this proved that all their negative comments were correct. "Black" was ugly. I no longer wanted to be in my skin. I desired to be much lighter. I thought, "God, why me? "It's not fair. If people didn't like their hair color, they dyed it. If people didn't like their weight, they'd lose it. If people didn't like their facial or body features, they'd change it. But not me. I couldn't change my skin.

"So, why am I stuck this way?"

Would I live this way forever? The brutal truth was yes! Yes, I would be dark-skinned until the day I died. No deep dream or magic trick would help me become any lighter.

Grandma was born in the early 1900s. During this era, the skin color of sharecroppers was used as a method of separation. Preferred treatment was given to the lighter-skinned sharecroppers. Darker-skinned African Americans, such as Grandma, were expected to stay outside and work in the fields. Naturally, dark-skinned sharecroppers envied this obvious division and the anger never escaped our culture. In fact, it remains a heated discussion in several African American households today.

Unfortunately, Grandma embraced the desire to have lighter skin. This mentality loitered on, and as Grandma took on the role to raise me, it was implanted without reasoning. She unconsciously embedded it into all her children.

As a child, as early as eight years old, I recall her saying, "Jhiree, all my kids are good looking. Of course, that includes you. BUT you all would look much better if you were light-skinned."

This statement, this very statement, dimmed my internal light. It was the first time that I realized something was wrong with my skin. She and I were the same complexion.

"Why would she say that?" Almost instantly, I wanted to prove to her that dark skin was nice, too! I made it my business to prove her wrong. Many nights, I fell asleep with this on my mind. I thought about how I'd look if I were light skinned. I constantly dreamed about how others would react.

I flipped through several television stations. To my disappointment, there weren't many dark-skinned actors or actresses. In disbelief, I started to pay closer attention to TV commercials. I could not find anyone with a dark complexion. Next, I searched through magazines and books, both in home and at school, and still . . . NOTHING!

"Grandma was right," I whispered to myself in defeat. "Everyone thinks that lighter skin is better and beautiful."

Summer visits to New Jersey only added to the traumatic experiences of North Carolina. The vitriol continued. Only it hurt much more when it came from the people that mattered most to me, my sisters. As a joke, they would reference my skin by saying, "You look like a black gorilla."

These words cut deep! I'd cry immediately and run off to be alone. Many times, I locked myself in the bathroom. I stared at myself in the mirror and wallowed in my tears. I wondered why I had been punished with such a dark complexion. My sisters did not know the amount of permanent damage they caused. Their voices echoed in my head at times of self-doubt. My sisters confirmed that my skin was ugly. Their harsh words were yet another validation that I was not beautiful.

I would be the "dark-skinned, cute-to-few girl. Forever!" I ranted.

Although high school was going well, it did not permit any relief. I was confronted with the insecurity once again. I had created a shield which would mask the hurt. I thought I fit in. I worked hard to hide the scars of my past and my sensitivity to my skin color.

Then one day, while at the lunch table with friends, a light-skinned, African American boy walked by and started hollering monkey sounds. Since I was in a group, I wanted to believe that the sounds weren't for me. However, they were familiar, as they resembled the sounds my sisters would make when teasing me. Just as planned, I ignored the negative behavior. I did not want to accept that this dark cloud had followed me into high school.

Later, while walking alone in the hallway, I came across that same kid. He yelled, "oooo, oooo, oooot, aaaaa-aaaaat," to mimic the sound of monkeys. This time, he looked directly at me and flapped his arms with hands in arm pits and said, "Hey, Blackie!" As others witnessed this, I was humiliated. But rather than running to the nearest bathroom to cry, as I'd done in the past, I decided that I'd pretend I was not bothered by his comment, not one bit. However, this didn't stop him from trying it again. My absence of a reaction decreased the level of attention from others around yet did not make him cease his attempts.

As not to disappoint, these words still crushed my soul. It was as if someone had stripped me of my clothes and there I stood, naked! Those two words had robbed me of my pride, dignity and self-worth.

Soon, I learned to laugh, too. I thought that would make the pain go away. At least bystanders wouldn't know how badly it hurt if I joined in. The problem is this reaction was not aligned with my truth. Though I had attempted the facade of being "unbothered," I'd return home, look in the mirror, and cry at the truth that was looking back at me.

As I matured, I accepted that I would never be as pretty as a lighter-skinned girl. I had to take a back seat. *I mean, at least when anyone decided to take a look in the dark-skinned pool, they'd think I was pretty*, I concluded.

Grandma hadn't made many adjustments. In fact, when I'd visit and we'd go out in public and a dark-skinned woman was well made up and spoke properly, she'd say, "She think she's something." I'd laugh along with her. But deep inside this comment and similar ones followed me throughout my life and were my "go-to's" when I felt insecure.

This was the one issue that I could not share with Grandma. She had confirmed several times without inquiry that she thought lighter skin was better. So, how could she console me or understand?

At difficult times like this, I needed my mom to comfort me. I yearned for the one person who created me to look me in my eyes and say, "Jhiree, you are beautiful. There is nothing wrong with your skin!" But addiction had stolen the validation I so badly desired.

Once I established what I actually needed to heal from the hurt, and I realized that the possibility of it coming from my mother was slim to none, I decided that in order to move forward in life I had to grow with my complexion. I had to work my magic to accent what God had given me!

Once I reached college, I learned that I had been experiencing something called "racism within my own race." Unfortunately, darker-skinned people within many races are faced with such verbal abuse and vitriol.

I promised myself that I'd strive to be the best "dark-skinned" girl that I could possibly be. I'd rock my skin well for all the other dark-skinned girls out there! To all my dark-skinned girls – You are BEAUTIFUL!

BLACK-SKIN

Black skin, black skin
What happened back then
I was just a kid,
embracing the features that God did
A motherless child, wasn't that harsh enough
Nope, people made life harder and overwhelmingly rough
Black skin, black skin
Had to constantly hear that I wasn't as pretty as my "light-
skinned" best friend
Mom's lost in her addiction
I'm lost searching for beauty from within
I can't find it nor can I find her
So I guess, I concur
Black skin, black skin
Life is far from fair
I was forced to live an awakened nightmare
Many days I wanted to scrape off this black skin, black skin
Trade it in to see what it was like to be a light skinned,
woman
Your color ain't cute, I'm told time after time

Mostly from people whose skin resembled mine
But you're pretty "to be" dark-skinned
They imply of surprise
Insult after insult, I just roll my damn eyes
Why won't they take my
Black skin, black skin
Tuck it into their ignorance

feel my humiliation and pain
Bundled all up into my fist
Sick of always defending this black skin that I'm in

Thought we've come so far, but when will it end
Yearned for a mom's love to help sort through this
confusion
But nothing trumps getting high
that was an obvious conclusion
My hurt and her addiction had no intrusion

SO...
Finally I'd embrace it
Shit I had to, cause I can't replace or erase it
Black Skin, Dope Skin, My Skin, Winnin
Black Girl Magic, yup Black...that Pure Melanin!

PERSEVERANCE

"**M**ommy, the college is requesting your tax documents so that I can apply for financial aid," I said full of excitement. "Girl, you better go ask your dad. I said I wanted at least one of my kids to graduate high school and you did! I don't care nothing about no college. You figure it out with your dad," she yelled in a voice filled with disdain.

College enabled me to escape situations that I had no control over. This is where I learned that my darker skin made me closer to my culture and, more importantly, my ancestors. This was the first step in embracing the beauty of my skin. Surprisingly, there were now many darker-skinned celebrities on television too. Throughout my college experience, no one seemed to care about anyone's complexion. Rather, it was about finding common interests in academics and extracurricular activities.

I lived on campus and the time away from home was needed. It rebooted my spirits enough to go back home to face my naked truths without having a mental breakdown.

When my college mentors from the Paterson Teachers for Tomorrow (PT4T) scholarship learned about my mother's absence due to her drug addiction, they were in shock! They found it difficult to believe that I had very little guidance in my household, and yet was figuring things out on my own. No one knew that I was shopping in the campus store for my little brother. I'd use my student card to buy him food and snacks because I didn't have cash. No one knew that I had missed several hours of sleep because I was up worried about where my mom was. And no one knew about the night I waited alone on campus for two hours after class for my mom, because I had lent her my very first car.

That night was scary. When she finally arrived, she was in tears. Once I got inside, she started to explain. She said she was late because she had loaned out my car to a drug dealer in exchange for crack cocaine. The dealer stripped my car completely of all electronics. A radio which once blasted my favorite music was gone, leaving only cut wires. It was a silent drive home. She cried of guilt and me of stupidity. I was so distraught that I stayed up late to complete class assignments. Finally, I attempted to fall asleep, but the salty tears prolonged it.

I maintained a convincing front for quite some time throughout my campus experience. My peers and professors had no clue of how complicated my life actually was because I did not allow it to bring me down. Nor, did I allow my mom's absence to cause me to miss any assignments or study for exams.

I was elected Most Noticeable Freshman on campus. Placed on the National Dean's List and inducted into several honor societies—all while maintaining the required GPA to sustain my full scholarship. I refused to let her addiction be an excuse for me to slack-off or a reason for people to pity me. Despite my mom's absence, I was loving the amazing person that I was transforming into.

REJECTION

"Jhiree, I've been meaning to tell you for several years that I'm getting tired of you going in and out of my refrigerator. You know where the store is, so go! I feel like I had to fill in for your mother's slack! See what happens the next time you go in my kitchen to cook or open my refrigerator," said the stepmom I had hoped would nurture and embrace me during my struggle to maintain a relationship with my mom.

These words were said as she shoved me out the doorway of her and my dad's apartment. I grew angry! My bottom lip felt heavier than usual. Enraged and hurt, I lifted my fist and prepared to hit her back. My huge belly made it difficult to make contact.

In the heat of my emotions, I had forgotten that I was seven months pregnant with my first baby girl. Before I could finally get in a hit, something grabbed my body. I was so furious that my feet left the floor and my body started levitating. I was ready to attack and defend myself no matter what. Suddenly my body came to a complete halt in midair. I looked back to see where the force was coming from. At that moment, I realized that I was not having an out-of-body experience. I was in Corey's arms.

He pulled me away because he knew that we could risk losing our baby. Unwillingly, I returned to my car. I punched my steering wheel several times. My feelings all raced for first place. All my doubts were right! She had never liked me! Pain rushed to the pit of my stomach. I was angry, hurt, and disappointed all at once. I wondered why yet another "mother figure" had disappointed me. This night confirmed the level of disdain that she had toward me. I learned she simply hated me because I was my dad's daughter.

That night, I decided it was best for both me and my unborn child to take a break from my dad's house.

Several days later, I received a call from my dad. He stated, "Jhiree, are you sitting down? I need to share something with you. Your grandma told me that my girlfriend wrote a ten-page letter about you. It is front and back. She sent it to your aunt and cousins down in Georgia. Everyone is upset!"

Tears gathered in my eyes, and as they overflowed, I thought, *Wow, look at the desperate measures this woman had taken to try to destroy me!* I wondered just how far she'd go. "What have I done to her for her to attack me with my own family?" I asked in disbelief. "Ten whole pages—well, twenty—what could she have said in that letter?"

Fortunately—and unfortunately—I never laid eyes on the letter. For quite some time, I felt distant from a family which was practically my second home. I was crushed because I knew the letter was created for revenge. Its content hurt my favorite people. I had no idea how to mend these threatened relationships. Conversations, holidays, and special occasions thereafter were awkward.

Nearly two years later, I learned that they were coming up to Jersey to visit. I had no idea how I planned to bring up the letter. I was determined to speak my truth. I wanted to take this opportunity to defend myself. I had faith that if only they heard me out, we could move past the turmoil that my dad's girlfriend had created.

One night prior to their visit, I spoke to God about how I should talk with them about the letter. I prayed that He would help me find the correct words to say.

As my dad turned onto their block, I became more and more anxious. I was not backing down though. I was committed to rekindling all relationships. I found courage because I knew that our love was too deep to let an outsider destroy it.

"Heyyy, everyone," I yelled as I greeted my family along with my daughter. I missed them so much! As I walked over to the empty space on the sofa, I hesitated to sit because everyone's voices started to echo. The room was circling around me. I hurried to sit and kept quiet because I did not want anyone to notice what was happening. Next, my pointer finger became numb. This continued until I had no feeling in my entire right hand. My tongue had a weird, tingling sensation.

Calm down! They love you! You can do this! I assured myself. I bit down on my tongue to see if I'd have a reaction to the pain, but there was nothing. It had become numb, too! I started to panic and was scared shitless. My heart raced. I had had enough! Finally, I tapped my dad, who sat closest to me on the sofa. He turned towards me and I attempted to speak but my words were slurred. Suddenly, he disappeared from my peripheral view and his voice stood alone. "I am calling the ambulance," my dad whispered.

I was both defeated and devastated. I did not get to address the letter. This was the start of what I learned would become my new "unwelcome friend" and next journey: Anxiety attacks.

Life seemed to never give me a break. My real mother was out chasing drugs and my supposed "stepmother" was out to destroy me. I started to believe that it was not meant for me to have a mother. Grandma's love would be it! I had to accept and move on.

MOTHERLESS ADULT

G raduation day was here! Tears of joy were met by flashbacks of all the events that my mom's horrific addiction had taken me through. As I wiped away my tears, I took a deep sigh, and realized that I was now a college graduate and ready to take on my career as a classroom teacher! My daughter was a little over a year old and my mom was back in recovery for about 4 months.

Shortly after I graduated, she and her husband decided to move to Johnstown, Pennsylvania where she rejoined the 12-step program of NA. Sadly, and similarly to our escape to NC, she relapsed two years later. As a full-blown addict, she once again returned to Paterson, NJ. My little brother remained in PA with his dad.

Two years into my career, one of the happiest days of my life had finally arrived. I had reached all weight loss goals and everyone was in place. Within hours, I'd marry my high school sweetheart. Butterflies crowded my empty stomach and I grew anxious for the "Big" moment.

"Jhiree, have you heard from Mommy?", my knee-baby sister, asked.

The glare in my eyes suddenly dulled as water filled them. My mom was present in all my wedding-day dreams. Since this was not my reality, her absence weighed heavily on my heart. I had to make many wedding decisions without her input. She didn't show for any of the dress-selection days, nor the fittings.

Just in case she showed up, I packed the dress which I had worn when I got crowned in high school. I was much thinner back then and knew the gown was guaranteed to fit her frail, thin body. I wanted her to look beautiful and as if she had been involved the entire time. I looked through the busy crowd of bridesmaids, past the photographer and videographer in hopes that she would come.

Finally, I tilted my head in silence afraid to let anyone know how distraught I was on my wedding day.

Before I could drop another tear, a faint voice whispered, "Baby girl!" It was my MOMMY! *God must've gotten tired of me begging that day.*

"Hi, Ma. OH, MY GOD, what happened to your face?"

"We'll talk about it later. Do you have something I can wear?", she asked, as she cried silently.

I replied, "Yes, Ma. Please ask someone to do your make up." As she walked away, what was once butterflies now felt like knives stabbing me in my stomach, killing one butterfly at a time. My focus was no longer about enjoying the "happiest" day of my life. I was redirected to devastation and hurt. I could only imagine what she had gone through before she arrived. I flinched as I thought of the person responsible for the damage done to her face. I hated her addiction! I worried just how many more moments it would steal from me. I prayed, "Dear God, I know you must be sick of hearing from me, but I know that You answer prayers, because Grandma said so. Could you just please, not let my mother die from this awful addiction? Oh and, God, . . . please allow the make-up artist to have the talent to cover her two black eyes. Please!"

PROFESSIONAL DISCOVERY

An addiction has the power to steal the most precious moments and milestones away from a family. Many times, forcing grudges, hate, and resentment amongst one another. The addict makes loved ones experience guilt, embarrassment, and discord. At times, the addiction becomes so disruptive that the family start to point the blame at one another. The family divides in to two separate teams that aren't necessarily even. Team one is the "enablers." Team two is the "tough lovers." The enablers constantly give in to the addict's wants and needs while the tough lovers have decided to purposefully not give in and has minimal exposure to the addict. The family starts to function in this dysfunction. Both teams attempt to persuade the other to join their side. In the meantime, holidays, birthdays, recitals, graduations, proposals, and weddings are sacrificed.

A BLESSING AND ANOTHER DEGREE

Our first child was four years old. Things were looking up, so my husband and I decided it was time for us to add to our family. For an entire year, we tried to get pregnant. After many failed attempts, I decided to refocus my energy and we laid the idea to rest. But, I had to do something.

I was five years into my teaching career and honestly, I felt that my drive to solely teach plateaued. I realized my concern for the "whole child" had grown and I was no longer able to ignore students sleeping in my class, asking for additional meals, or their crying spells. Although we were forced to constantly move forward with the curriculum and prepare our students for assessments, I desired to learn more about their lives. My childhood experiences provided an extra layer of empathy for these students. I needed to help! A plan was needed.

I learned very early in life about the benefits of planning. My mom's inability to fulfill her promises or maintain our household taught me this. I planned so much that I had a plan C for my plan C, just in case the original plan C didn't work out. Since I lacked control over my mother's addiction, I would pride myself in managing all other aspects of my life. Creating a plan gave me control over a situation.

Committed to my passion of helping my students, I decided to go back to school for a master's degree in Professional Counseling. I applied to two universities and after taking their entrance assessments, was accepted to both. The program that I accepted offered a dual certification in both School Counseling and Mental Health. I was ecstatic! Not only would I be able to assist the students, I would also now have an opportunity to counsel adults and families in a private setting!

But this light was almost immediately dimmed. Feelings of self-doubt and unworthiness crept in. At this point, no one in my family had obtained a master's degree. So, who was I to even attempt?

I had no one to ask. *Should I be afraid? Is this a bad idea?* I questioned myself. This would have been the perfect time for my mom to have stepped in with encouraging words. But I had no way to locate her.

Suddenly, I remembered the same strength that I had found when I registered for undergrad school. I got through it! I realized that my mom's absence had increased my ability to adapt and survive in unfamiliar terrain. *I did it then and I could do it now,* I exclaimed! These positive thoughts immediately decreased the volume of my negative self-talk. I registered!

Approximately two weeks after I was accepted, I learned I was pregnant. "Really? Now? What great timing!" I thought sarcastically. While my husband and I were overjoyed to finally be pregnant, I knew the journey ahead would be rough.

But I was ready for the ride!

I had to inform the department chair at the university that I was pregnant. I recall feeling like a fifteen-year-old who had to break the news to my parents. I was nervous, to say the least.

"Are you sure you can do this? You may want to take one semester off and then come back," was the department chair's response.

Game on! I thought. She had no clue how driven I was. Anytime someone doubted me or told me I couldn't do something, it ignited a fire deep inside that made me strive to prove them wrong.

Needless to say, I ended my second semester super pregnant and with a 4.0 GPA! I later graduated with two high honors.

PROFESSIONAL DISCOVERY

In my experience, I have learned that in every negative situation, there is a positive waiting to be revealed. Initially, the clouds are way too thick to see through, but as you sleep on the situation and reevaluate from a different perspective, you will discover this positive. It is important to speak nicely to yourself throughout the process. Allow your feelings to fluctuate and embrace them as they come. However, it is imperative to identify the positive or lesson learned. This breakthrough could help you accept a promotion, be brave, or motivate you to work even harder.

SECONDARY TRAUMA

S everal years into my career, after giving birth to my second daughter, I started to not only mourn the relationship that I had missed with my mom but, I also mourned the relationship that my girls would miss with my mom, their grandmother. At times, I'm envious of the relationship my mom had during her sober years with my nieces and nephews. My children have not had the opportunity to experience that "Grandma Rita." Grandma Rita spoiled every single grandchild. She not only bought them everything they wanted, but she was present. She attended their school plays, dance lessons, and events. It truly saddens me that my kids missed out and have only been exposed to the "I-need-a Arita."

My children have seen her beaten up. They have also witnessed her asking for money, food, and clothes. Sometimes, they ask, "Mommy, why are you so mean to Gramma?" They don't understand, and I am made to look like the bad guy. I do not let them see the tears behind my frustration. They don't know how hard it is for me to tell my mom she can't come sleep over at our house, because I'm afraid she'll steal our things and sell them. They don't know how many nights I've waited for them to fall asleep so that I could cry myself to sleep, worried about her.

They DON'T KNOW!

At least, that's what I hope and pray. The thought of them ever worrying saddens me. The pathology would continue, and another generation would be affected by my mom's addiction. My children would remember me chasing my mom, who's chasing drugs.

As their mother, this upset me because I realized that I had *no* control over her addiction. I didn't ask to be a part of it, and I definitely did not want my children exposed to or affected by it. Addiction sucks, and it's not fair. It causes so much hurt for all the innocent people who are closest to the target.

I have tried to do everything right in life or at least to the best of my ability. I've given my kids things and experiences that I didn't have. I've gone to their shows and have given extra hugs and kisses on days when I'm the one who really needed it. I strive to give them stability. I want to be, for them, the mother I never had!

As an adult, I still needed her advice on "adult things." She was not around to answer questions about purchasing a home, organizing my finances, parenting, or what's it's like to be a wife.

I'm sure her influence could have avoided so many of my trial and error experiences. But she was never around for me and that hurts. If I dig a little deeper, I'm lonely. The tears build up as they are right now and I question, "God, why did addiction have to take my mom? Why does this have to be my story?"

I constantly questioned when and if she'd ever stop.

An even scarier question was, "Will her heart stop before she does?" I lived daily with this torturing thought.

The idea dangling at arm's length, "Here's your mom. You want her? Maybe she'll get better, maybe she won't." I lived life not on a daily basis, but on an hour-to-hour basis, worrying about receiving that call.

I'd always turn to Grandma Cherry for a little glimpse of hope. She would say, "Mmm-Mmm-mmm," while shaking her head. Although, we were on the phone, I knew her mannerisms very well. "Jhiree, I don't know what to say about that Rita. Girl, I can't say much 'cause I don't know what it's like to have a momma out there on that stuff. Rita better quit this here mess. She's getting too old. You hang in there now, ya hear. Continue to pray for God to take away the taste. 'Cause only HE can.", she said. My silence would always let her know that I was on the other end of the phone, crying. "Jhiree? You hear me, chal'?"

"Yes, Grandma, I hear you," I'd reply in a somber voice filled with disappointment, defeat, and hopelessness.

Throughout my entire life, even up until this present moment, I've dealt with broken promises from my mom. What makes me most upset is that the hurt of three-year-old Jhiree versus the hurt of this thirty-five-year-old Jhiree hasn't changed. Every single time I've helped her check into a rehab facility, I think, *This is it!* I honestly believe that I would get my mom back. I desperately yearn to live life as a "normal" functioning family. I'm naive and hopeful!

This hope angers me.

"Why was I so desperate for her sobriety? Why won't I just give up?"

I'd pray so hard, like Grandma said, for God to take away her desire to crave drugs. But each time, I was disappointed. By now, I've memorized her routine. On days one and two of detox, when no one else was allowed to use the phone, she would somehow manage to call me twenty times, literally. She gives me her list of necessities, which is EVERYTHING because she's always homeless prior to going in. I then stop my entire life to shop for her list of items and would deliver them right away. The following day, she'd start complaining that someone is bothering her. Then finally, the calls stop and I'm driving along the streets she frequents and there she is!

Here's the part that disappointments me the most! No matter how many times she does this, each time is as if someone throws a bowling ball at my stomach. Immediately tears begin to fall. Next, I feel angry, but not at her. I'm angry at myself for crying and caring.

"Why do I continue to stand in line for this roller coaster ride when I am terrified? Why do I believe in a person who has lost hope for herself?" I questioned.

It was time for some deep soul searching and healing for myself.

DREAM VACATIONS

I always knew that once I was old enough, I'd somehow thank my grandma for all she had done for me. She was my solid foundation and my only reference of normalcy. If it weren't for her, I do not know where I would have ended up. She continued loving me even on days when I disliked her. No words nor amount of money could ever repay her for the time, love, and dedication that she had given me. I realized that she was completely done raising her children—yet she chose to start all over with me.

Throughout my childhood, she and I traveled up and down Highway 95 two or three times a year. She loved to travel, so I asked, "Grandma, if you could go anywhere in the world, where would you go?"

She replied, "Hollay-wood!" As her laughter grew obnoxiously louder and louder, she banged her fist against the arm of the sofa and kicked her heels deep into the carpeted floors.

Ohh, I'd give anything to hear that laugh one more time.

"Well, pack your bags, 'cause we're heading to Hollywood!" I said.

The look on her face was priceless. She couldn't believe that she would actually visit Hollywood. Prior to now, it had always been a dream. "Chal' we're gonna be walking down them der streets and walk right into a super star!" she said comically, as she grinned ear to ear.

Shortly after, I kept my promise and was on a flight to meet my dad, Grandma, and my oldest cousin in Hollywood! We went on a tour to visit the homes of superstars, took photos next to the stars with famous people's names on them, and frequented the restaurants that the Hollywood stars had gone to.

I learned that no one had visited Vegas, and thought, "What the hell, we might as well go!" And so, we did! I drove all the way there. About three and half hours of desert and conversation. Grandma had an amazing time! She loved all the lights and said they reminded her of "Up the Road"— meaning, Time Square in New York City.

"God-almighty-knows, Ol' Jhiree done it again!" she said with excitement.

I smiled. "Anything for you, Grandma! Where should we go next?" I inquired.

"TEXAS!" she yelled. "Chil' I can't wait to see them cowboys on those horses! It'll be just like the westerns with Chuck Norris," she said all googly-eyed and bushy-tailed. My dad and I chuckled at how cute and naive she was to think that Texas would be the actual set from her favorite western television show. Neither of us was brave enough to challenge her imagination.

We arrived in Dallas, Texas and I immediately asked the hotel clerk, "Ma'am where do we find the cowboys?" She pointed us in the direction of their collection of visitor's brochures and said, "Dallas, Fort Worth" with a thick, southern, welcoming accent. We got settled into our rooms and the very next morning we headed out to Fort Worth. I prayed a cowboy would ride past us on a horse. I knew that would make her day! To our surprise, they did!

We all bought cowboy hats and waved at the cowboys as they put on their show. Once the show ended, Grandma posed with the cowboys to take photos. She was in awe.

"Jhiree gal, you really outdone yourself, ya hear!" she said.

"Where to next?" I asked.

"MEXICO!" she screamed, as she stomped her foot into the ground and laughed.

Aligning with her excitement, I yelled, "Okay, let's go! We'll need to start working on getting your passport."

"Aww, shy now," she stated in disbelief and excitement.

In the midst of planning Grandma's dream vacations, guilt occupied my heart. I constantly reflected on how badly I wished I could do the same things for my mom. But, how could I?

ONE MORE DAY OF FUN...

Please pick me up, everyone hates me out here,
My mommy's voice trembled of hopelessness and fear
Again, I spread my cape to go be superwoman
Failing to realize the only person who can
save her is that ONE Man
I thought she'd finally reached her rock bottom
Instead she stares at me like I'm the problem
Guess I didn't come fast enough, just drop all my plans and
rush, rush, rush
Grandma'd say ain't much I can do just pray
HE takes the taste away
But I rush to her aid every time anyway
who knows today might be *MY* lucky day.

Saying the word *MY* only implies what some try to deny
but this *IS* my struggle as well
I swear this woman and her addictions
have put me through pure hell
Even still, giving up on her is not an option
I go into fright or flight while others are watching
No matter how many times she fails,
I say, goodbye Mom, I'm proud of you and
I pray you get well.

People immediately doubt the seriousness of her attempts
Meanwhile I'm smiling and saying
thank God she even went
But not this time, I arrive, and her words were in a slur
She looked a little dizzy like her vision was in a blur

I shook my head of hurt, pain, anger and disappointment
Fought to keep my feelings inside so she didn't see me
lose my shit

Aloud I said,
Mom I love you and at that moment tears begun
She barely looked me in the eyes and said,
"Jhiree, I promise I'm almost done."

She smiled and said, "I just need one more day of fun"
Does she realize one more day of fun
could turn out to be her very last one!
Drove away, guess I'll wait 'til her day of fun is done
I cried, spirit died, once again the stupid addiction had won

SUPER-DAUGHTER TO THE RESCUE

By this time, Mom was homeless and had to do whatever she could to survive as an addict. She had been arrested several times for stealing from stores and panhandling. Since my stepfather and little brother lived in PA, she moved about freely and had very little responsibility. She found no purpose in becoming sober.

I hadn't totally given up on her though. I was finally an adult and thought I had the power to save her. I searched and searched for rehabilitation centers, but she would barely complete the mandated three-day detox. Other times, she'd stay a little over a week before signing herself out. Every time she would check herself into a facility, I was naively hopeful and relieved. And then, like clockwork, I was notified by the social worker that she had left.

This cycle grew to be so exhausting and painful. Many times, my husband found me lying on my bedroom floor in a fetal position, crying hysterically. "What didn't I do right?" I'd say to him, as he consoled me. "Maybe if I would have bought the items she requested sooner, she would have stayed in the detox. I should have purchased nicer clothes for her. I should have returned her calls faster."

I blamed myself every time she was unsuccessful at treatment. Her failure was my failure. I was determined to find a place that would help her. I had to! I was on a mission to fix my mom. I knew it would all be worth it when she was sober. I yearned for days we'd go out for brunch together. I wanted so badly for my children to spend quality time with their grandma. In my eyes, they had never met the "real" Rita. My heart broke even more for them. I envisioned the day we'd be on vacation on some island laughing about the days of her addiction.

With every failed attempt of sobriety came the deferment of these hopes.

I did not like that people called her a crackhead. Sure, that was who they saw, but they did not know my mom. My mom was the person that always gave away money to family and friends. Crack cocaine made her become the person who now begged for money. My mom once owned her own home, and now she's sleeping on the steps of public places. I wanted everyone to see her bounce back yet trying to save her was draining me and compromising my own mental health.

Seemed my life had regressed and her behaviors resembled all of those from my traumatic childhood. Only this time, I was privy to her addiction firsthand. I was the passenger and she was the driver. As the passenger, I went in the direction that she intended. I ran when she wanted me to and stopped when there was no request. After several years of being in that passenger seat, I learned her routine. She'd promise to detox as a means to manipulate me to give her exactly what she wanted. At her request, I'd take her to detox. The caveat, however, was that she'd say that the hospital would not accept her unless there was alcohol and drugs in her system. So, I'd have to stop at the liquor store, purchase a beer and cigarettes and then drive her there. Shortly after, she'd be right back in the streets. I became exhausted with all the failed attempts to cure her addiction. I learned that many times, as soon as I was out of sight, she'd catch the bus right back to town. The excursion was merely an attempt to get a drink and cigarettes! See, I was the parent and she was the rebelling child.

I wished so badly to find the courage to shut her out. It would make life much easier! But my connection to her was undeniably that of a loving and compassionate daughter. I chose to join forces and fight the addiction with her!

Unfortunately, this decision would enlist me as an involuntary yet volunteered "first responder."

One could only fathom the gruesome events that I've witnessed. Journaling was my relief when none could be found. It was the calm in the midst of my horrific world of chasing my mom's addiction. By this time, I was living what many would call "my best life." I was now a School Counselor and had a second career as a Licensed Counselor, working in a private practice. I had a master's degree, two beautiful daughters, married to my high school sweetheart, and we were home-owners. Yet, I lacked fulfillment and happiness solely because I was unable to cure my mom's addiction. This realization created the desire to know more about myself. Why was I choosing to take on this responsibility? What landed me here? What patterns, choices, exposure, raising, or religious influences led me to believe that this was my task? Journaling provided a space for me to manage and process it all.

Here are a few entries from those devastating experiences:

Unknown Number

3/5/2017

Today, I received a call from an unknown number. While most people would quickly hit the ignore button, I looked forward to answering these calls. I would become upset and anxious if I missed one. My mom would ask total strangers to use their phones to call me. Some preferred calling for her, as they feared she'd steal their phones. Others would let her call, but hurried her to get off, because they were in route to their destination. Nevertheless, they'd call me, and I was grateful.

Guilt and anxiety would urge me to answer these calls every single time.

"Umm, umm, Hello!" My answer to each call was always rushed, as I constantly worried if that last person who beat her before had resurfaced. Visions of them trying to kill her drowned my mind.

"Hola!" said the voice on the other end of the line. It was my mommy! She'd always start her calls this way, and though I was excited to hear her voice, I would quickly get upset because I wished she was actually calling to see how I was doing.

"Yes, Ma," I'd always say, trying to keep a caring tone through my annoyance. I struggled with mixed emotions *every time* she called. I didn't know whether I'd have to drop what I was doing and run to her aid or if she'd have some story to tell me about how someone did her wrong. She'd have situation after situation with other addicts who were also homeless. *Wow, homeless, I can't believe I just said my mom is homeless.* Voicing this currently sends waves of nausea to my stomach.

"Baby girl, someone took my shoes! Can you please bring me some now? I'm standing on Broadway in front of the grocery store. Hurry, baby girl!" she yelled frantically into the phone.

This is my mom's rock bottom. No matter how bad she's gotten in the past, she's always maintained her appearance and an apartment. But not anymore.

Many nights, as I lay cuddled in bed next to my husband, I wondered where she was sleeping. Especially on extremely cold, snowy, or rainy nights. But what could I do? I had driven her to her boyfriend's house several times to escape the addiction. Although it was two hours away, she'd steal from him and come right back.

I had taken her to hospitals over forty times. As soon as she'd get her disability funds applied to her card, she'd sign herself out. I concluded that her stay in any rehab facility relied heavily on how close it was to the fourth of the month. I saved myself a lot of energy once I realized that her strategy was to go in about a week prior to receiving her check. I was all out of ideas.

Once, I allowed her to stay at my place. Nearly one week later, I found out that she was using drugs in my bathroom. I had to ask her to leave. The idea of kicking my mom out made me feel terrible. But, what could I do? I couldn't allow her to endanger my children's lives. Therefore, staying with me was no longer an option. I exited my thoughts and hurried to bring her shoes.

Drastic Measures!

5/12/2017

As a last resort, desperate to help my mom, I did the unthinkable. I wrote a letter to a popular television show. This show films the life of the addict and then gives them an ultimatum to attend a rehabilitation center. If they refuse to attend, their family members and close friends promise to cut ties. I was confident that they could help. I feared for my mother's life. My life was consumed by thoughts of her overdosing or of someone killing her. Here's what I wrote:

> *Please, please help* my fifty-five-year-old mother. *She Is Going To Die!* She's gone from 185 lbs. to 98 lbs. in one year! She's been homeless for the past year and has robbed me, family members, and stores. She's been beaten badly, hospitalized for walking in the street naked, and arrested several times! I have photos (that will not upload) and videos. I'm tired of the anxiety, stress, heartache, and fear that she causes me! *PLEASE* help save my mommy's life! She used to be such a beautiful woman. I can't take it anymore. I don't know what else to do. On my

wedding day, we had to cover two black eyes with make-up for her to be in the wedding because she was beaten the night before. As I cry writing this shaking, and my heart pounding, this is my last option. I have *faith that God* will answer me! You are that answer. I've taken her to detoxes, shelters, and every hospital's mental unit! I don't know what else to do. My heart is *broken!*

After we were denied for the show, I was furious! I vowed never to watch it again. They had become the place to direct my anger. I was exhausted and frustrated, yet again. Helplessness transitioned to hopelessness. I was out of ideas. All I knew was that I wanted my mommy back! But not this one. I yearned for my once sober and nurturing mom. Her addiction was far too big for me to fight alone.

The Fight

8/22/2017

Days never get easier. The more I tried to separate myself, the harder social media worked to connect me. People recording the scene and laughing while they go live. Never caring whose mother, sister, father, child, aunt, or uncle they're laughing at. My stomach cringes. Tears gather in the corners of my eyes and feel heavy. As I struggle to keep my eyes open, they begin to burn.

I want to watch because I need to know how bad they hurt her, but I don't want to see my mom getting beat up. One woman, three times her size comes out of nowhere and begins punching her. Blows directly to the head, one after another. I reach for a Kleenex to stop the salty tears from entering my mouth. I'm in disbelief and can't take watching it anymore.

"She's going to die soon," I whisper. "Someone is going to kill her. This is the worse she's ever been. Can't she see it's causing everyone so much stress?"

My phone rings, and I pause the video. It's my sister asking if I've seen it. I look up. It's only 8:31a.m.

Is this really the start of my day? When I wake up, I pray, say good morning to everyone and tell them to have a good day. Little did I know, my day would start this way. My sister starts to watch. She's angry and upset too. I shake my head and together we say, "Wow!"

Double Trouble

11/28/17

Unfortunately, my oldest sister followed in my mom's fractured footsteps. She also became addicted to crack cocaine. I grew more upset with her rather than empathetic. The thought of her joining my mother's addiction and habits was gut wrenching. She knew the effects of addiction and what we had gone through as a result. Why would she consider this drug?

The school day started as usual. Bell rang, all students rushed to their homerooms. The morning announcements began. I turned on my office computer. While waiting, because it takes *forever* to boot up, I received a missed call from my second-to-oldest sister. I decided to ignore it. Besides, she knows that I'm at work and most of the time it's something that can wait until I'm out. As I proceeded to log into the computer, I noticed another missed call from her. This time, I began to worry.

"She never calls back to back like this," I say aloud.

Adrenaline rushed through me as I hurried to call her back. After several attempts, she answered. Now, this is the sister that talks really fast. Emergencies only increase this speed. I struggled to understand what she was saying. Finally, after I replayed what she had said several times in my head, I thought I understood. I repeated it back to her for clarification and hoped that I had heard it incorrectly.

"Did you say that there is a video circulating the net with our oldest sister getting beat up?"

"Yes!" she replied frantically. "It happened like ten minutes ago. I'll send it to you now!"

I immediately started to panic. I'd now be forced to watch another traumatizing video. As I waited for it to appear on my phone, I prayed to God that she was okay. "What if she's been beaten like mommy," I thought. "What if she's lying there waiting for one of us to come rescue her? What if she's dead?"

An alert popped up and I quickly pressed play. As I watched, my heart sank. Tears fell down my face. I immediately jumped into my sister's body. As she and I became one, I felt every punch that was served to her by the masculine woman in a hunter green coat. We kept yelling, "Please stop, stop hitting me!" As I yelled in my office alone, another bell rang. I realized it was time for me to pull it together. I had a group of children waiting for me. I paused the video and quickly transitioned back into my own body.

I tried my very best to center myself and refocus. I mean, I was at work, but tears continued to fall. I looked in the mirror and whispered, "Pull it together, girl." I was so disappointed in myself and in my reaction. I started to tremble and cry aloud. There I sat alone weeping and weeping.

I thought to myself, "Why do I have to go through this with the two closest people in my life?" I had already suffered enough. Life shouldn't be this difficult. I've done everything by the book. So why? Will I be punished my entire life?"

These thoughts were interrupted as the video of my sister replayed in my mind. I then hit play once more on my phone in hopes of getting a clue of her location. I finally admitted to myself that there was no way I could continue this workday as if things were "normal."

The idea of my sister being only a few blocks away from where I was sitting and me going on with my workday didn't sit well. My sister needed me. I packed up and hurried to her rescue. Then, moments after I had already left work, my uncle called. "I found your sister. She's okay. You want to speak with her?"

My heart raced. "Oh, my gosh. Thanks so much, Uncle."

"Yes, of course!" he stated.

"Hey, little sis, do you have any money? I just need like two or three dollars," my sister pleaded.

Yup, seems she's totally fine, I thought.

PROFESSIONAL DISCOVERY

Children who are raised with a parent who is addicted to drugs or alcohol are more likely to inherit a genetic predisposition. They are at a higher risk to develop an addiction. A parent's inability to cope encourages their children to seek ways to mask their issues as well. As a result, this modeled avoidance behavior is adopted. Coping skills aren't taught and the children are left to rely heavily on a substance in overwhelming situations or experiences.

This particular insight allowed me to empathize with my sister's condition. However, the anguish of witnessing her in the same state as our mom did not lessen the pain.

Tough Love-Soft Heart

1/3/2018

Nearly ten years into my mom's straight run with addiction, she decided to give me the nickname "baby girl," since I was the youngest of her four daughters.

I thought it awkward to obtain a nickname this late in life, but quickly learned it was much easier to just go with the flow. Shortly after its creation, I despised the name. Seems she used it as a source of manipulation. It meant I was "special." But only "special" enough to write down her laundry lists of things she wanted. She knew that I was the only one who would assist, immediately.

When I would explain that I didn't have what she was asking for, she would say, "So, you going to make me go out here and sell myself to make money? Okay, fine!" She knew these words would create a path for her to get her way. Shortly after I made the connection, I decided I'd no longer be manipulated. Rather, I'd call her out on it and continue to do my best when I was needed. I prayed she wouldn't have to do any "favors"; however, if she chose to, it had absolutely nothing to do with me.

"Baby girl! I'm hungry, I haven't eaten since yesterday; can you bring me something to eat? Please! Hurry."

"Okay, Ma, where are you?" I responded.

"I'll be by the public library! Baby girl, hurry, please! I'm sick!" she yelled.

"Okay, give me thirty minutes and I'll be there," I replied and hung up.

Once again, I found myself trying to pick and choose my battles. There was no way I was going to leave my mom hungry.

But I also knew I'd have to hear my husband's concerns. "Jhiree, I know you love your mom, but you can't keep stressing over her. You cannot keep running every time she calls. She has to want better for herself. I keep telling you to stop going in that area. It's dangerous and people are learning who you are. You never know what those people will do to you – to get back at her!"

While everything my husband said was definitely a possibility, I knew he couldn't understand what I was feeling. He had no clue what it was like to have a parent dealing with an addiction. He had never experienced this. Why should I listen to him? Although he stood right in front of me, my mom's voice echoed much louder. I would never knowingly leave her hungry.

Contrary to his desires, I hurried to her rescue. This same fight caused more and more distance in our marriage. I hated feeling like I had to choose between my mom and my husband, but she was hungry.

I quickly grabbed her some pizza, but when I pulled up to the public library, my mom was no place in sight. I decided to park and wait. I thought maybe she was on her way. At the edge of my peripheral vision, a bright red baby stroller caught my attention. There it sat, alone on the steps of the library. "Did someone abandon their baby?" I thought. Next to the stroller, on top of a flat cement surface, there was what appeared to be a blanket. I shrugged and thought, *Maybe someone had been lying there and left their belongings.* Right, that's it. No real surprise there. This was pretty normal in this area. After about fifteen minutes of waiting, I grew anxious. Impatient, I decided to get out of the car to see if I recognized any of the items. Nothing looked familiar.

Suddenly, I heard a sound. It seemed as if someone was snoring. As I turned toward the sound, I noticed that the snoring was coming from a person beneath the blanket. I tapped on the sleeping body.

"Excuse me," I said softly, and thought, *Geesh, they're really thin.* The blanket had only a few lumps in it. Immediately, the snoring stopped, and the person repositioned themselves as to obtain comfort. This shift revealed the top half of their face. However, they did not awake.

"Mommy!" I yelled. There she was, lying on the concrete, sound asleep, as if she were on her living room sofa and fell asleep watching TV. My heart was broken and ached terribly. I felt ashamed, guilty, helpless, embarrassed, disappointed, afraid, and relieved all at once. Questions sprouted like weeds in my mind. *Why my mommy? When will this ever end?*

I wanted more than anything to take her to my home and allow her to stay with me. She's my mommy! She belongs to me! Tears slid down, creeping into my sealed, trembling, lips of frustration. At this age, she should be in her own home, enjoying retirement. This stupid addiction ruined my mom's life and I hated it! My mom should be baking cookies and spoiling her grandkids. Anywhere but here. I found myself staring at her for a long period of time in disbelief that this was her reality— our reality.

"I've got to take her to my home. She's going to die out here!" I whispered to myself. Almost instantly, I reflected on the last time we lived together and the constant chaos. She'd steal my belongings, and then sell them to get high. She'd also tell any and everyone our address. At times, they'd pick her up from my home. Once, she returned home and said we needed to give her money because she owed it to someone that was threatening her and waiting outside. So, the thought of taking her to my home in this condition was totally unacceptable and no longer an option.

I made a tough decision and promised myself that I would no longer allow this type of dysfunction into my home. But I had to do something. I couldn't let her stay here, on the library steps.

Suddenly, my thoughts grew lucid, tears dried up, and I sighed deeply as reality settled in. I noticed that I hadn't been breathing. Rather, I was processing and thinking. I paused and took several deep breaths. They were so deep that my shoulders transitioned up and down. I felt my stomach contract. I embraced positive self-talk and said to myself, *Duh, Jhiree, remember the definition of insanity is doing the same things over and over again and expecting different results? Who was she fooling?*

"She's not ready," I concluded. My focus shifted. I begin to think as a mom to my own children first, and a daughter second. I realized I could not constantly expose my children to her lifestyle.

I quickly wiped away the residue of the newly formed tears. I didn't want her to see me crying.

"Mommy! Mommy, get up. I brought your food." As I tapped her, she opened her eyes and looked around as if she had forgotten where she was. She pulled herself into an upright posture and placed the pizza on her lap. I looked down at her feet and noticed she had on bedroom slippers.

"Ma, how do you fall sleep out here like this?" I inquired. "It's two in the afternoon. What makes you comfortable enough to close your eyes out here with so much going on?"

She replied, "I got nowhere else to go."

Normally, this statement would be over-whelming. It was a sure way to break me down and I would cry. But not this time. This time, I quickly refuted her. I replied, "That's not true. You need help! You've stolen from every family member that's allowed you to sleep over. You've got to do something!" I shouted out of frustration.

"Then take me to the hospital!" she replied of defeat. "I'll do detox, and then long term."

Now, that was my weak spot. She asked for help. Tears settled in my eyes once more, but this time they were tears of joy. This was exactly what I needed to hear. It made no difference that she had done this exact same thing at least twenty-five times before. I was excited every single time. I prayed that this was the one time she would change. I wanted my mommy back!

As we drove to the hospital, she started to make the usual promises. For my stability, I learned to protect my heart and I allowed her to go on and on without any expectations.

As I waved goodbye, I sighed. It felt as if a weight had been lifted from my shoulders. Finally, I knew exactly where she was. Even if she didn't stay long, at least it was a break!

Airforce

1/12/18

As I sit here on a plane getting closer to my baby brother's basic training graduation for the Airforce, rather than having feelings of excitement, my chest aches because I know that he will want my mom's presence. Yet the man he's become will not allow him to express that desire. My heart hurts not only for him but for my mom as well. I can only imagine how she must feel right now. Had she been under the influence of drugs or alcohol this morning when we met up, I'd know she was masking these feelings. But today is a sober day for her. Although I don't know exactly what that means, in my mind, I believe it's the hours that addicts are able to feel. It's the hours that pull them back into the desire of becoming numb of it all, once again. I wonder how she feels knowing that her son is graduating from the Air Force and she will not be there?

"She can't go because she doesn't have an ID." I repeated her response aloud to myself. "What a lame excuse," I thought. Well, for the average person. But for her, the addict that she has become and the homeless lifestyle she lives, it's an acceptable excuse. Today must be a reminder of just how low she's gotten.

She called several times. "Baby girl, I wrote baby boy a letter. Please stop by before you head to the airport. I need some money and food, and a wig, too."

"Oh boy," I thought. "Here goes 'I-need-a.'" This was the nickname I had given her, because every time she calls, she has a long wish list. "I need this, and I need that."

I wasn't sure if I wanted to entertain her drama. I wanted badly to get the letter for my brother, but I did not want to look her in the face and tell her that I was not going to fulfill her wish list. I've never gotten any pleasure out of telling her that I don't have anything. I've finally learned how and when to deal with my mom because her addiction is dangerously draining to me. Some days, if I feel I have the energy, I go help out. But on other days, on days when I know I'll break down, as tempting as it is to go save her, I go home. I used to feel guilty about it, but I now realize I have to choose me.

As my sister, *"the knee baby,"* and I approached the field where the basic training graduation was taking place, we began running as I did not want to miss a second of this sentimental moment. As we stood for the National Anthem my nose tingled and I could no longer fight back my tears. Through all adversities, my little brother made it! I was overjoyed!

I GIVE UP

Destined to lose her battle from my beginning
Her addiction looks at me while grinning
Addictions have no heart
They destroy rapidly and rip families apart
Is she now possessed
Because selling your body means your pride is gone at best
Some will do anything for their next high,
even sacrificing the secrecy between their thigh.
Where's my mom? Are any parts of her left
If the answer is yes, it must be in distress.

I'd like to find that little light inside, hug it tightly against
my chest
Tell her the run is over and watch her rest
I love her so much, but she doesn't care
My love isn't enough
she's high
looks through my eyes
and gives a blank stare
No matter how high I achieve
her addiction weakens me
I had no right
This isn't my fight
I accept that I have no control
But I am forced to watch life snatched from her poor soul
her once healthy and beautiful body fading away
I pray each detox visit she'd stay
yet it's always the same exact ending
The addiction is persistent and we're back at the beginning

Yasssss!

6/5/2018

Woke up this morning and was definitely feeling myself. Music pumping, my fancy sunglasses on—which brings many compliments—and I'm pretty proud of my outfit selection today. I'm not driving the car of my dreams but at this moment it's feeling like I am. I'm high off life! Woooo—Weeeee! I woke up and I've nearly reached work on time. Won't He do it?

I start my victory dance, which is right on beat to Mary Mary's song, "Shackles" that I'm listening to. I'm nearly two blocks from work. The light was yellow, and I contemplated whether to breeze through it or exercise my brakes. With plenty of time to spare, I decided to stop.

"Go, me!" I pull down my sunglasses and wink at myself in the rear-view mirror. Morning's great and I'm following the rules! "Yasssss!" I praise myself in the mirror.

As I'm sitting at the light, I noticed someone lying on the concrete near the entrance of a Dunkin Donuts. Beside them lay their sorrows, worries, addictions, and pain all wrapped up in grocery and black trash bags. The person appeared to be sleeping comfortably with a blanket covering them while lying on the filthy ground.

Suddenly, the volume of my music lowered and Mary Mary's voices were distant. The party that I had created in my mind came to a screeching halt. My entire ego flew out the passenger window, which I had cracked a little to let others experience my music. My forehead began to feel weird. There was this abnormal pressure present. I removed my sunglasses of confidence to get a better view.

"Is that Mommy?" I said aloud.

I then turned the music completely off because it was interfering with my vision. The sound of the traffic and the music quickly converted to noise.

"Geesh, how long does this light take to change?" I anxiously awaited the light to turn green so I could get a little closer. I needed to see if this person was my mommy. I never took my eyes off the person, as I prayed he or she would move a little so I'd get a better view.

Honk, honk! "Move lady! The light's green!" yelled the irate driver right behind me.

I wondered how long the light had been green, because he flew past, giving a "move-the-hell-out-the-way" beep. The kind where you press down on the horn and hold it!

All this commotion must have disturbed the person lying on the ground. They sat up and started to look around.

"It's a man! Whew, it's not Mommy," I said, with a sigh of relief. My adrenaline instantly decreased. I began to feel my muscles unstiffen one by one. I looked over at the time and realized I had exactly five minutes to swipe in at work. I made the left turn and headed toward the parking lot.

"The Call"

7/16/2018

Today, while clothes shopping, I received a phone call. On the other end was a frantic voice. "Ma'am, I know you do not know me, but I was walking down the street and I noticed your mom, Rita. She needs your help—please come! How soon can you get here? She needs an ambulance!"

Immediately, my heart started pounding and tears filled my eyes. I could only imagine what she'd say next. Finally, words slipped from my lips in response, but not much beyond saying, "Yes, that's my mom."

"She's been beaten unrecognizably; please come to help her, please!" the woman screamed, her voice trembling. "She's lying on the ground on Broadway, across from the Board of Health. Hurry!"

As I ended the call, the aisles of the store became blurry and voices faded. I envisioned a photographer and snapshots of my mom lying on the ground, covered in blood, taken from different angles. The next image had a group of people kicking and pounding her body. As the final flash occurred, I snapped out of it.

I quickly handed all items to the customer service counter and rushed down Route 80. I wanted to assure my mom that no matter her faults, I'd always be there to help and comfort her. The fact that she was able to give my number to this woman indicated to me that there had been some brain activity. But I feared what would be left of it by the time I reached her.

Questions crowded my mind. How long had she been there? Were people just stepping over her? Who did this? What on earth could she have ever done to anyone to deserve this?"

But this wasn't new to me. No, no. This exact scenario and similar versions have played out repeatedly in my head over the past sixteen years, with this call always being my worst nightmare.

As I grew closer to the scene, I spotted a white blanket. There lay my mom on the cement steps of the entrance to an abandoned building. As she lay with her eyes closed, a sigh of relief happened. She looked as if she were at peace and would be laid to rest soon. The fight of her life would finally be over; and she'd no longer have to suffer. We would no longer have to suffer. I would no longer have to anticipate this scene. This exact scene.

These feelings battled with: *What if this is her rock bottom? What if this is a wakeup call? Maybe this would force her to stay clean.*

As I moved further from my thoughts and drew closer to my reality, I noticed food surrounded her as it once did when she'd make us hefty Sunday dinners. Flies landed on her body and bloody wounds. Her left eye was swollen shut and a knot the size of a golf ball covered the left eyebrow. Dried-up blood that once poured down her face now stood still. Her nostrils were sealed with dried-up blood as well. As the flies surrounded her, I moved in closer to fan them away. I did not even want a fly to harm her. I noticed the tray of food had a scripture attached. I attempted to read it but was unable to because the flies then swarmed around me. I grew confused at whether the flies had interest in the food next to her head or the revealed flesh that peeked through several parts of her face. Either way, they weren't going away.

Hello Passport; Bye, Bye, Mexico

9/20/18

Okay, so this element of my life is one that's most devastating.

I promised myself that I would commit to journaling about it on a day where I felt stable and strong. A day when everything else was going well and I could handle the overflow of emotions that would surface. As I'm writing now, I worry that I'm not ready, yet again. My heart hurts and I can feel its exact shape. It's as if it's outlined and stands alone while the remainder of my body is numb.

My grandma was my life! I promised God that I'd take care of her as she once took care of me. Losing her would be my greatest fear.

Who would I call when I needed guidance? Who would I call when I needed nothing except to hear her voice? Who would I talk to prior to my departures for my trips, and once I arrived? Although I lived in New Jersey and she in North Carolina, everyone knew they could call her to learn my location.

When I attended funerals, I would say a long prayer to God: "Dear God, please, please don't take away my grandma. She's my best friend, my second mom, and my biggest cheerleader. Please God, skip her. I'm not ready!"

Truth was . . . I would never be ready! Today marks about two and a half years after this event and I have finally found the courage.

So, here it goes . . .

"Hello . . . oh, hey, Grandma," I said and smiled. It was always nice to hear her voice. "It's here!" she exclaimed. "I can't stand this here picture, but I reckon it'll do. I finally got a passport!" she yelled as she laughed.

"Awesome! Let's get this vacay started!" I hollered back.

About one week into our planning, during our routine Sunday, pre-church calls, Grandma explained to me that her doctor discovered a benign polyp on her colon. She stated she was scheduled to do a very minor surgery to remove it the next week. She told me the procedure would only require two-to-three two-inch incisions. Still, my body grew tense. I was silent.

"Jhiree, you still there?" I confirmed that I was and repeated the information she had shared for accuracy. Then, I hurried off the phone so that I could share this news with the family. Although she made no big stink about it, I was worried. She was eighty-one years old, and this would be her very first surgery. Someone needed to be there. I wanted to be there!

A pause was placed on our Mexico trip. I booked my flight to arrive the day before she was discharged from the hospital.

February 3, 2015. A date I will always remember. The date of Grandma's surgery to remove the "very small benign polyp." Turns out that midway through the procedure, the doctors discovered that the polyp was actually cancerous, and it had spread throughout her stomach. They thought it best to remove the cancer during the surgery, although we had not given consent. Grandma woke in the Intensive Care Unit (ICU) with a stapled incision that stretched from beneath her breast all the way down to her waist. The moment I learned that she was comfortable enough to speak, I called the hospital room. I felt both excited that she had made it out alive and heartbroken because someone had to break the news to her about the cancer.

"Who is this? Is this my mechanic? Is my car done yet?" Grandma yelled into the phone.

With my eyes full of tears, I said, "No, Grandma, this is Jhiree."

"Who?" she asked, with a voice of uncertainty and confused.

At that moment, I yearned to be the mechanic, because at least she knew who he was. I adjusted my shoulders, because they instantly grew heavy. I buried my face into the palms of my hands, because I didn't want my two daughters to see me crying. A thump in my belly reminded me that I was pregnant. A gentle reminder that increased my tears.

"Grandma had no idea . . ."

I had only two days until I could embrace her. It seemed that time had stopped because these were the longest two days ever. I planned to share the pregnancy with her as soon as we laid eyes on one another. Though she admired my girls, she'd be ecstatic when she learned that I was having a baby boy!

Finally, I arrived. The closer I got to Grandma's room, the more anxious I became. My palms were sweating and all the negative head junk, which I had talked myself out of on the flight in, had resurfaced.

What if she doesn't recognize me? What if she looks terrible?

I worried whether she had already been told that the doctors found cancer in her stomach during the surgery.

"Wait, cancer . . . is this really happening? Does my grandma have cancer?" I said this aloud in disbelief. She was in prime shape the last I saw her. Still driving her own car, still cooking, and still being my best friend.

"How on earth did we end up here?" I whispered to my brokenhearted self. My dad and I embraced one another and together we sobbed in tears of disbelief. It had all happened way too fast. As my dad wiped away my tears, he explained that the doctors said her temporary inability to recognize us was due to dementia commonly developed by the elderly after a major surgery. He updated me on her medical status and prepped me for her physical appearance. Hand in hand, we entered her room.

"Hi Jhiree," Grandma said, but not in her normal bubbly, obnoxious voice. Rather her voice was one of defeat and doubt. I hadn't seen her like this before. It seemed her faith had been snatched away. "Chal' you reckon we gon' make it to Mexico?" she asked. She spoke as if she had given up.

"Yes, of course, Grandma," I stated with certainty and a forced smile. The thought of her not making the trip saddened my soul. Mexico had now become my dream vacation as well.

"The doctor says he'll schedule your chemo around our trip," I said to comfort her.

"Oh, well . . . okay," she replied and turned to stare out of the window of her ICU room.

The next day, Grandma was discharged. As we gathered her things, it seemed that her spirit had been uplifted. In fact, she yelled, "I took a licking, but I'm still ticking!" This meant that the surgery was a big hit; yet she survived it and was ready to move on. She attempted to laugh aloud, but the incision made it difficult, so she settled for a giggle. I made sure she was settled back into her home, and then headed to the airport to return to New Jersey.

The flight back was one of silence. I realized that I was so distracted by her condition that I forgot to mention my pregnancy. I lost myself in the clouds reminiscing about life's lessons, words of wisdom, and special moments shared with Grandma. I'd smile at the memories, while crying in fear of us not gaining anymore.

Eight days after I returned home, my dad called.

"Jhiree, your grandma isn't doing too well. I'm here with her at the hospital. She's been refusing to eat or drink since she returned home. She was readmitted to the hospital this morning." His tone was low and filled with hopelessness.

My heart fell to my stomach. Something didn't feel right. My dad was a man of integrity and strength. This guy on the phone sounded almost like a weeping, doubtful, helpless child.

I needed to be there!

I searched for flights, then buses, and finally, I decided to drive.

I called my dad to share these plans. "Daddy, I'll be there tomorrow," I said. I wanted to give him a huge hug. Yet I feared seeing my grandma so sick and the thought of having to say goodbye caused immense pain in my chest.

"Jhiree, there's no need for you to panic. I'm sure she'll be fine. They need to run more tests. Just hold tight," he said.

Hold tight?

I couldn't. I hated so badly that I was miles and miles away. I wished there was a magic spell that could have instantly placed me there with them.

The following day, my dad called me again from the hospital room. This time, there were familiar voices in the background. He said my great aunts were in from out of town. They were my grandma's sisters. This only increased my anxiety. Why were they there?

I decided to video chat so I could properly assess the room. I paid close attention to everyone's non-verbal body language. I got a sense that they were not being honest about the extent of her condition so as to not worry me. I then realized that video chatting into the room was probably one of the best, or worst, decisions of my life. There lay my grandma's body, all dried out. Her physical appearance looked as if the life had been sucked out of her. She had had so many pokes and procedures.

It was now eighteen days since her initial surgery. By now, she should be recovering. Instead, she's readmitted, and doctors are trying this and that. She looked weak and tired. Really tired.

Several hours later, I received the call . . . the one that I had prayed and prayed for God to prepare me for. . . the call I had dreaded my entire life.

"Your grandma took her last breath, her heart stopped. She's resting now, Jhiree. She's with God," my aunt said. I dropped the phone. Every moment after the sound of the phone hitting the floor is a blur.

The beautiful gold and white casket cradled Grandma gently. A purse she and I had recently purchased lay next to her, unclutched. As the casket slowly closed, so did our story, and just before they sealed it shut, a piece of me quickly flew in with her. At that very moment, my life became unfamiliar. There I sat, holding her passport, as my tears wet the pages.

UNCLUTCHED PURSE

A purse unclutched
An obnoxious laugh hushed
A memory to reflect
A lifetime unmet
A passport unstamped
My life in contempt
No more dream vacations
Gone from me without explanation
Hands stiff
An angel lay next to my last gift
My heart broken
Many words left unspoken
A beautiful soul laid to rest
She gave me her absolute best
Sobbing of pain
A lifeless body remains
A mother's love I'll never forget
A bond created with no regret
Lost in this unfamiliar world
God now has my number one girl
I wish this were all an awful dream
Without her, what does this life even mean
Her final signature now embedded forever on my forearm
There I reflect, smile, and at times still mourn

Grandma took a trip that surpassed Mexico. She had gone to a place that she had sung about her whole life. It was a trip that I could not have planned. Although, it was one of her dream vacations, it was one that she had to travel alone. My energy would now shift to "fixing" my mom.

Professional Discovery

Losing a loved one can turn your world upside down. It is one of the most painful and stressful experiences that you may ever encounter. You cannot see—nor do you desire— a life without him or her. Completing your daily activities becomes overwhelming and frustrating. You try, but restructuring your life is difficult and almost impossible. Grieving occurs for both the loss of the physical person and for any hopes that you had for a future with that person. Some days you are fine and other days you cannot seem to pick yourself up. You struggle to keep it together for those around you. The truth is that your loved one will not be replaced, and you may not ever "get over it" which is okay. To all experiencing such, grief therapy teaches you how to reshape your life and reflect positively on the times that you shared with the person. I encourage you to pursue counseling.

Umbrella Day

4/30/19

Today's weather was pretty ugly. It was what I like to refer to as "an umbrella day."

I never liked umbrella days because they required me to actually use an umbrella. I preferred lighter rain where I'd just run.

As I opened the door to exit my work, I stepped into a huge puddle of water. Though I was frustrated by the amount of water in my shoes, thoughts of my mom surfaced. I worried if she was someplace dry. I knew that nothing, no form of precipitation—not rain, sleet, hail, or snow—would keep her from securing a way to get her next high. I envisioned her drenched in water, standing alone on this dreary umbrella day.

Rather than rushing to my car to escape the rain, I began walking slowly in hopes of spotting her in the streets. But for what? What would I actually do if I were to see her? I can't take her to my home. It's now too late for the daily check-in at the women's shelter. She's burned her bridges with all family members who once opened their homes to her. "So, what could I do if I bumped into her?", I questioned to myself.

I then thought maybe I should start running.

"Wait, who runs from their mother?" I said aloud, but only for myself to hear. I grew ashamed. I started to question my own morals and values. "Ugh!" Such a draining experience and she's not even present. As I got into the driver's seat of my van, I thought, "What a waste of adrenaline!"

Finally, I pulled off and began to head home. Back to my nest of comfort I had worked so hard to create. It was my escape from it all! I looked forward to entering my home and having my children bombard me with their daily happenings at school. As I was driving home, I began to imagine my "Lil Monster" running up to me, grabbing my legs, nearly knocking me to the floor. I couldn't wait!

I dreaded the short, but long, drive on my way home through the area where drug addicts of all sorts hung out. I always prayed I wouldn't get the red traffic light in that area. When I wasn't so lucky, addicts surrounded my van like kittens during feeding time. They would come up to the car, asking for money.

Suddenly, I noticed a very thin woman with a hood on and no umbrella going from car to car. It seemed she was asking for something. One of the cars refused to roll down the window. I thought, "Wow, poor woman!" and shook my head. As I got closer, my heart grew warm, but not in a cozy way, more like the burn experience from indigestion. I started driving slowly and lowered my window to get a clear view. I didn't lower it all the way because the rain was falling harder by this time. I yelled out, "Maaaaa!" She immediately ducked her head down, and so did I. I believe she and I both shared disappointments in her behavior. Sometimes I worry about who's hearing me call out "Ma"! Other times, it's not even a concern. It is what it is. I only have one mother. This is mine!

Mother's Day

5/12/19

It was the night before Mother's Day. I was folding clothes when I suddenly realized I hadn't spoken to my mom in over a week. Prior to this year, she'd call at least once every two to three days. But lately, she's gone over a week without calling.

Every year, the women in my family would get together and celebrate Mother's Day while "the husbands" spent the day with the children. This had become our tradition. Once gathered at the table, we'd all laugh about how difficult it was for us to get out of the house. We'd have to change one last diaper, leave notes for the husbands to follow, or answer one million questions from our kids. It was a holiday I looked forward to. My mom's attendance had always been questionable. I had finally gotten used to it.

Special days like this reminded me of what I did not have. Not only did I not have her today, I hadn't had her for quite some time. The addiction had her. It spent not only holidays with her, but every day with her. It had become the most important thing to her. Nothing else mattered.

First Responder

6/7/2019

It was a pretty smooth Sunday. Though I was a bit tired from braiding both the girls' hair, it had been an altogether, relaxed day. The kids were asleep, and I decided to take a longer-than-usual steaming shower. Google was playing some of my favorite R&B hits from the 90s and I was in my zone, I swear! Singing off key and doing all the throwback dances. Suddenly my shower karaoke was interrupted by the ringing of my phone. I stepped out quickly and answered.

"Hello!" An unfamiliar voice yelled through the phone.

"Hi, yes, who is this?" I asked.

The voice continued, "Your mother, Rita, gave me this number. You're her daughter, right?"

"Yes", I responded hesitantly.

"Listen, we called the ambulance twice and they are not coming. Can you please come to get her? She's been stabbed badly and needs to go to the hospital now! We're standing outside of the library on Broadway, across the street from the chicken store. We will wait here with her until you get here. You on your way?" he asked desperately.

I explained that I had just gotten out the shower and I'd be there as quickly as possible. My mind was racing a hundred miles per second. I had no time to think! I quickly threw on some clothes and grabbed a sheet from the linen closet. I tossed it over my passenger seat and sped off. As I rushed through the streets of Paterson, which had now become her home, tears piled up. I feared her condition and did not know what I would encounter once I arrived. *Wait, could this be a setup? Was I crazy for going alone? Is this her ending?* I thought to myself. I imagined blood oozing from her body and me holding her in my arms as she took her last breath. All of these thoughts, yet not one of them changed the direction that I was driving. I was determined to be there for her. If not me, then who? I pulled up to the location to find my mom hunched over, crying and yelling an agonizing scream of pain. Her left and right arms securely around the necks of the men carrying her into my van. Door shut and we were off to the hospital. The ride over was one of tears—mine silent and hers echoing through her torturous holler. It was a cry that I will never forget.

"I don't want to die!" she yelled repeatedly, pressing her hands tightly over the blood pouring from the wounds.

We pulled up to the emergency room, and a crew rushed out to remove her from the van. I parked quickly and entered the ER, but my mom was nowhere in sight. "All ER doctors, please report to triage immediately," someone announced repeatedly over the intercom. I feared they were calling all these doctors for my mom and she had taken a turn for the worse. Approximately six hours later, she was released to the Intensive Care Unit. By this time, my sister—the second to the oldest—had arrived and she and I walked in to see our bandaged-up mom. Doctors explained that they had to do more incisions to ensure there was no internal bleeding. They explained she'd need about three to four days to recover.

As I drove out of the ER parking lot, I glanced over at my passenger seat. My once-white, beautiful sheet now covered with my mommy's blood confirmed that this was not a horrific nightmare. . .. Instead, it was indeed my reality.

On her second day of recovery in the ICU, I learned that my mom had signed herself out of the hospital . . . against doctors' orders.

PROFESSIONAL DISCOVERY

The Power of Journaling

Journaling provides a space for non-judgmental creative expression. If you are angry, it's your opportunity to yell and swear without anyone knowing. It serves as a method to either release negative tension or praise yourself without guilt. It allows you freedom to say all things that may be misperceived otherwise. Thoughts are free to roam as they come and there is no need to defend them. Allow your feelings to guide your writing and just go with the flow. There is no right or wrong. You are in control!

Reflecting over your writing will allow you to connect dots and shed light on common practices in your life that lands you in a specific condition. Journaling is where manifestation begins! It is a place to share your most frightening dreams and aspirations! Whether you choose to journal for ten minutes or two hours, writing is healing, and you will reap its benefits.

PART 3

Healing

Self*-Actualization:* Powerless yet Empowered

To all my readers who have dealt with a parent, spouse, close friend, family member, or sibling battling an addiction, please save yourselves before you attempt to save the addict. No matter how difficult the situation may be, **always choose you**! You get to decide when to expose yourself to their illness. Don't live life in guilt because you cannot respond to their every need at every moment. Rather, live life knowing that they are in your heart and you have given all you could without sparing yourself or your quality of life. The choices they've made are theirs and do not diminish nor affect your self-worth. Don't just live life in the shadow of an addict's choices . . . focus on designing your life.

FREE

I've decided to let life take its course
Recovery isn't easy and hurts worse when it's forced
Dangerously high hopes of regaining my mom

Devastation arising time after time
It took years of stress, humiliation, and pain
So today I stand tall and release myself of the blame

I must move on, For I am my own nurturer
While trying to save her, I was my own murderer

Done feeling guilty for the life I've created
I've been shown favor, so Jesus I'll take it!

Who am I kidding
she's having all the fun
Taking risk after risk
high and intentionally numb

I must love me first for my own self-care
It is what it is . . . life ain't always fair

Finally I give up, I've thrown in the towel
I deserve it all, I've made a new vow

Choosing me, me, me,
Unapologetically

So I'll keep her sober spirit alive
Relieved I reached this conclusion
I survived!

Life's amazing, it's time to enjoy
with my two beautiful daughters and my one little boy

I am her
She lives in me
Every time I look in the mirror
I find her nice and healthy
I must take care of the Rita inside of me
Because only she can truly make me happy

Deep sigh,
tear in eye,
a glimpse of hope,
but far more doubt,
wondering when,
she's alive within,
I put down my pen,
explored all options,
not doing that again,
Ahhhh, finally, I've created an end!

"PERSONAL" DISCOVERY

In hindsight, I realize that I had accepted my mom's addiction into my life with open arms! I became accustomed to there being drama and adversities throughout my path and subconsciously chose to continue to impose such experiences onto myself and my family. I allowed the fear of her death to dictate my life. I had to let it go! I realized that it was not in my physical powers to cure her addiction. I had to make peace with myself and bare no guilt for where her addiction lands her.

As I reflect, I realize I soared at times when others couldn't understand it. Many times, I could not even understand it.

When I finally surrendered and separated myself from her addiction, I reflected over my journal. Although, some pages brought tears of sadness, others gave me a sense of pride because I had grown so much! Some pages made me laugh while others made me cry. As I closed my journal, I smiled.

I lifted my head and discovered that God had been setting me up the entire time! His plan was to use my experiences to touch the lives of others!

THOUGHT I WAS MADE TO STRUGGLE

Life has this funny way of not allowing you to plan it
At times it's so rough, your head's spinning and you
question if you're on another planet

Everything's falling apart and into place at
the same exact time
You cannot pinpoint the reason nor identify the rhyme

You'd like to make sense of it,
but your money isn't adding up
You've built a foundation although it was rough
You have doubt since you're the first to experience such

The problem is that there isn't a problem,
You're just so use to trying to solve them

Sadly, you question if this comfortable life is meant for you
Is it all too good to be true?

Will this be short-lived,
and they'll all point and laugh at you

Always remember what God has for you is for You

Without a mom to second it,
you question if this new life is true

They say you have a gift, count your blessings,
but you're still searching because its buried beneath
all the old habits of stressing

Never give up, no matter the struggle, keep pressing
For in every good moral there's a learned life lesson

PROFESSIONAL DISCOVERY

Life's traumatic experiences have a sure way of knocking us off our feet when we least expect it. Embarrassment, guilt, and denial block our vision to see a way past the residue and emotional baggage surrounding the trauma. This inability causes depression, withdrawal, isolation, and hopelessness. During these difficult times, we are most vulnerable and desire a way out.

Vulnerability is the space that welcomes the most growth. It's the place where you're willing to let down your defense walls and allow another person to learn who you really are. It's where your deep-rooted issues lie. The state of vulnerability helps you discover who you are today and how you arrived here.

I encourage you to please seek professional support to discover and create a solid plan to help elevate you from the traumatic experience. Therapy is a safe place to explore your being, systemically. It identifies patterns and triggers which you may not have noticed otherwise. Therapy inspires you to view issues from a wider perspective and to make connections. It empowers you to persevere through issues that may not even be of your own, such as a loved one's addiction.

You are not broken, just bent! Your "bounce back" awaits you!

MY THERAPEUTIC ADVICE

You've got to start "filling" yourself
so you can start "feeling" yourself.

While we have no control over other's actions, we have complete control of our reactions. Once we've mastered how to manipulate a device, a car, a remote, any device, we become comfortable pressing the buttons and expecting a certain outcome. We learn what's acceptable or unacceptable (the buttons). What's considered beauty and thus praised, and what's considered ugly.

What happens to these devices if we take the batteries out? They lose their functions, right? Therefore, we can press the buttons, but nothing will happen. You see, the batteries are what powers the item.

Truth is, the world may be a harsh place to live; however, you must choose to pull the batteries out of your insecurities or situations—whether it be your skin complexion, a body feature, an accent, a physical impairment, trauma, an addiction, or a disability. You must face these challenges head on and remove the reaction that you've given in the past.

This takes away their power to degrade you or make you feel unworthy. Once others learn that the buttons no longer work, they will have to find their next target. But guess what, it will not be you!

Asking someone else to be responsible for, maintain, or create your happiness isn't fair. Most of the time, we're asking this of people who are not happy themselves. Therefore, they are unaware of how to make you feel an emotion they've not experienced.

Don't SHOULD all over yourself!

You have the power of choice. You can choose to follow your heart or choose to follow your mind. Both are coming from within and are options. Hindsight is 20/20. Always make the best choice, at that very moment, and one that you will not regret.

Fear

The fear of rehashing and revealing personal pain surrounding my mom's addiction kept me from sharing my story. If I can touch just one life with my experiences, then I'll feel it was worth it. So many people believe they're out in this world alone, but the truth is someone is either currently going through or has gone through what you are experiencing. I encourage you to be brave and share your story unapologetically! It belongs to you.

Take control!

You may be at a point in your life where you feel you are no longer useful to society. Some of you may have considered suicide or have had unsuccessful attempts. You may feel that life has failed you numerous times. You may be suffering from depression or anxiety or have been a victim of traumatic forms of abuse: mentally, sexually, or physically. Please know that although these events were severely painful and have had lasting impacts on your life, they are only a *part* of your story. They do not define who you are or where life will take you. Do not allow those experiences to control the direction of your future.

In life, you will learn that many issues aren't your own. Rather, they have fallen in your path and you've attached yourself to them. Give them back to their owners! Take control. If you are reading this book, you are already one step ahead of your circumstances. You've already decided to choose life. You're already seeking opportunities to become a better you.

Congratulations! You're on the way! You're no longer just "thinking." This is the first step to many more accomplishments.

Let all of life's *tests* be your *test*imony. Cherish your story and the struggles faced because it is through those struggles that you became who you are. Continue to choose you and put yourself first. When you look around, you will appreciate life's accomplishments and blessings because you understand the pain it took to get there.

Be grateful, humble, and caring because you can relate to those who are less fortunate. The main difference between a homeless addict and me is that I've decided to not allow my circumstance to win. I took the harder route of growing through negative experiences and so can you!

I am in control! You are in control!

Make a commitment to yourself and stick to it!

In academia, we write papers for grades. I was determined to treat the writing of this book as such. Rather than there being a letter grade, I was empowered by the idea of my life's experiences connecting with others out there who have suffered the effects of addiction by association.

I decided to treat the completion of this book as an assignment . . . due to me. I even assigned a due date!

In the work force, we are committed to putting our all into accomplishing someone else's goal or deadline. Imagine what would happen if you put that same energy into completing something that you are passionate about? Some idea that you've dreamed about in great detail. One that you think deeply about while taking a shower, reading a book, or watching a TV show.

Procrastination and fear are our two greatest enemies! Kick their butts by acting on your big idea! Invest in building your empire! Commit time for you to plan and manifest your vision!

Sometimes, this means we must turn off reality TV, social media, and family demands to focus on ourselves.

Invest in You!

"Investing in name brands will not increase your self-worth but investing in you will add to the brand of your name!"

Name brands do not increase your self-worth. They are facades and create illusions.

When you reach home and you're stripped of all the outer world influences, what do you have to offer you? Are you happy with who you are? Do you know who you are? Are these **your** personal values or have you been taught or influenced to believe that these items increase or enhance your worth?

Create a mantra. One that you will chant at times that you are feeling discouraged or powerless.

Here's mine:

*I don't strive to be like the Joneses
because I am the Joneses.*

This enabled me to see that being me is good enough! I don't have to be anyone else. You can only strive to be "your best you"!

Here's a list of quotes that I've created to help you shift the focus from your loved one battling with their addictions back to yourself. Please add these to your repertoire of daily affirmations and positive "self-talk"!

1. Persevere until vision is clear.
2. Today's a fresh start! Yesterday's over! Tomorrow is not promised!

3. Let people's doubts be the flame of your fire and your success be the proof of your pudding.

4. 3Fs: Allow your Fear to create your Faith and your faith to embrace your Future.

5. Everything happens for a reason, It's all a part of God's Divine Plan. Learn to trust it and go where He leads you!

6. You can't make a promise to your past, but you can make a commitment to your future.

7. Though we cannot predict the weather, we can prepare for the storm.

8. Don't forget to LIVE your life.

Let's start your healing process TODAY! Complete the attached *Workbook Activities!*

MY BRIGHT FUTURE JOURNAL

Journaling Activities

Use the companion journal to complete the following activities. If you do not have one, please feel free to use a personal journal or contact me to purchase a *My Bright Future Journal.*

The remainder of the journal is for you to write about experiences that resonate on a daily basis.

I would love to hear how journaling has impacted your life.

Please share with me via:
MyCurrentPast@gmail.com
www.AuthorJhiree.com

ACTIVITY 1

Have you identified what happiness is for you?
What does it look like? What does it consist of?
Please complete in your journal.

I challenge you to write these things down. Next to each, write ways in which you will fulfill this happiness on your own. For example, I love massages, so I would put massage on my list. Next to that I'd write: schedule one every two months.

It's imperative to write a realistic approach of how you will accomplish these goals. Otherwise, it becomes overwhelming and creates yet another disappointment.

As children, we're taught to love others and be nice to and respect others. We're taught: "If you don't have anything nice to say, don't say anything at all." However, we aren't taught to invest in and love ourselves.

Many times, we fear choosing ourselves because it's frowned upon and can be perceived as being selfish and narcissistic. Forget about them—you've thought about them far too much! Feel no guilt in choosing you. Now let's define your, "Happy".

ACTIVITY 2

Take a look at yourself and find at least three positive things to say to yourself daily and record in your journal for an entire week.

Accept compliments without criticizing yourself. I've been guilty of this many times. Someone will go out of their way to say, "I love your dress" and right away, I'd reply, "What, this old thing? I've had it for six years!"

Remember that we teach others how we want to be treated. A negative or self-deprecating response may deter future compliments. It's okay to simply say, "Thank you!" and accept the compliment. This approach is welcoming rather than dismissive. More than likely they'll keep the compliments coming. I love the warm feeling of being recognized. How about you?

ACTIVITY 3

List 10 Positive Escapes in your journal.

When reality gets to be too hard, find something positive to be your escape. This can include a book, exercise, a new experience, binge-watching a show, listening to some throwback music, or spending quality time with friends. You deserve a break! Make it happen!

ACTIVITY 4

Challenge yourself to hold a conversation with someone that you wouldn't normally speak to and journal your experience. What were you experiencing internally? Did you have any preconceived notions?

I firmly believe that all people in this world have gifts! Something that they can teach you. A way that they can impact your life, thoughts, or beliefs. People have so much to offer!

In life, as you encounter people, whether a homeless person, someone less fortunate, or someone of equal importance, I want you to ask yourself one question: What can I learn from them? Every encounter serves a purpose. Don't miss your blessing by not hearing them out. Never think you are better than or above someone. We can always use growth and insight! Their life's experiences have entitled them to possess something unique.

Sometimes we ignore others' presence because life is too busy. We're constantly on the go. But what if they've got the missing piece to your puzzle and you choose to count them out? It's your loss.

Everyone, at some point created dreams, goals, and aspirations. Whether they were successful at accomplishing them is irrelevant. What's important is their journey—the forks in the road, the struggles, or the traumatic events that derailed that dream. Maybe their story will help you avoid similar situations. Maybe their story will resonate with you because you haven't stopped to see how fortunate you are. Though this activity may be a challenge, please note that discomfort leads to success. You got this!

Testimony of Thanks

Thank you, Mommy, for bringing me into this world. Although you've battled with your addiction for most of my life, please know that I love you with all my heart. Your addiction has taught me several life lessons. It has prepared me for life's ups, downs, and disappointments. I know that you have a wonderful and kind soul and my real mommy lives deep within you. She is awaiting another opportunity to debut.

Love, Your "Baby Girl"

To my dad: Thank you for being the best role model that a little girl could have ever asked for! You taught me the value of education. You are one of my best friends. We laugh together, cry together, and crack jokes together. I will forever cherish our "Bonnie and Clyde" father/daughter excursions. You are the perfect example of what a father should be. You were my tour guide, lead or backup singer, and biggest supporter. Thank you for trying to make my life as "normal" as possible. Lastly, thanks for making me go to church on days I didn't want to as a teenager. God has really shown me favor! Love, Your #1 Daddy's Girl

To Grandma Cherry (God rest her soul): Thanks for taking me in and raising me as your own. Thank you for never giving up on me and for listening to my good and bad days. I am forever grateful for everything you did for me! I hope I've made you proud! I will carry your name on in my psychotherapy practice *Cherry Blossom Healing,* which was inspired by you! So many times, I've picked up the phone to call you, only to feel my heart break again. I think about you every day. I find peace in knowing that heaven truly gained an angel. Love, Jhiree

Acknowledgements

To my high school sweetheart and husband, Corey Sr.: Thank you for stepping in with the children and ALL household duties when I was on yet another adventure or mission to become a better me! You still give me butterflies and I love you more now than ever!

To my first-born, Zoreya: You're smart but I'm still the genius. I truly admire the young lady that you have become. Sometimes, when you aren't watching, I stare at you and shed a few tears, because I realize how blessed I am to be your mother. You are strong-minded and confident! No matter what anyone says, you're comfortable with who you are. I recall when you were just five years old, I questioned why you'd always cling to me around other people, even family. With your little hands on your hip, you instantly replied, "Mommy, this is who I am and I'm okay with it. Other people have to be, too." I was speechless. Please continue to respectfully stand your ground and live your truth! I'm ready for the rollercoaster ride called "teenage years." So, bring it on!

Love, Mommy

To my middle child Zya: You inspire me daily! You keep me on my toes with your beautiful smile and charismatic spirit. One day, while driving, you said, "Mommy, why are you always looking for your mommy? It reminds me of the book, *Are you my mommy,* by Dr. Seuss." THANKS, Zya for always telling it like it is! You are amazing, smart, and super caring!

Love, Mommy

To my baby, Corey Jr., my first son: I like to call you my "SONshine"! I thank God every day for blessing me with you. You are bright and so full of energy! Little boy, you are my twin and I just love watching you grow. I work very, very hard, so thanks for always forcing me to play even harder! Can't wait to see the intelligent and handsome man you will become.

Love, Mommy

To all my siblings: You were my first best friends! I love you Retha, Tisha, Dinka, Lil Calvin, Lil Jerry, Bryan, Aundre, Brianna, Nettie, Sheron, Keith, Marc, Michael, Andres, Nikki, and Ke'ara. We miss you Calvin Jr.! Heaven truly gained a comical angel.

To Grandma Bernice: You will forever live on in my heart. Your unique personality, sayings, and humor was one of a kind! I love and miss you!

To my mother in law: There isn't a person I trusted more with my babies! Thanks for being the best Nana ever!

To my best friend Akia, I am so grateful for our friendship and thank God for placing you in my life that freshman summer of EOF. You made me laugh my way through the tough times! Love you Gwah!

To my Comadre Maria and family: Thanks so much for stepping in when I needed you all the most. You are such a beautiful family and I am forever grateful!

To my PT4T family, Dr. Hill, Dr. Gillette, Ian, Nancy, and to all my friends in both Paterson, NJ and Fayetteville, NC I've built lasting relationships with: Thanks so much for your friendships, unconditional love, and guidance. You may not know it, but on my darkest days, when I felt left out, hurt, angry, inadequate, guilty, and unwanted, you were my motivation to keep pushing! If it weren't for you taking the time to listen to me, I do not know where I would be. Especially, the ones of thirty-plus years: Leandra, Danielle, and Pauletta. Thank You, Thank You! You all will forever hold special places in my heart.

To my mentor: There isn't enough words that can qualify or quantify your guidance and support. You are truly an inspiration and I am forever grateful for the impact that you have had on my life. Thank you!

To my best friend since high school, Meggan: Though we're miles apart, our connection is extremely unmatched. Ihay ovelay ouyay urlgay! You right, you ain't wrong! Looking forward to your new book! I'll have my dictionary and thesaurus on hand! Love you girlie!

To my best friend, Leyda, whom I met in undergraduate college: I've learned I cannot share my visions with you because you will definitely hold me to them! You are a friend who has taken my dreams as your own and when I'm exhausted in my tasks, you will not hesitate to pick them up. I thank God for our friendship and love you like a sister!

To my best friend, Sanya, who I immediately connected with in graduate school: Thanks for presenting me with countless opportunities. Thank you for making things that I thought were unattainable, reachable. You and Alfonsina are my personal therapists, my shoulders to cry on, my biggest supporters, and the ones to provide me a kick in the behind, on the rare occasion that I need one! I love you ladies to pieces.

Special thanks to my family! You all were the village that I needed to become the person that I am today!

About the Author

Jhiree Davis-Jones is a National Certified Counselor, a Middle School Counselor, and a Licensed Professional Counselor (LPC). She is the owner of a private counseling practice named after her Grandma Cherry—*Cherry Blossom Healing, LLC*—located in Paramus, New Jersey.

Wife to her high school sweetheart, Jhiree believes her greatest blessing is the opportunity to be an amazing mother to her three beautiful children. Jhiree's professional passion is discovering diverse methods to enhance her life and the lives of others; sharing her concepts/insights as a motivational speaker, and advocate for self-care awareness.

Her mantra is, *one should always secure a Plan C for Plan C, just in case the original Plan C doesn't work out.*

Driven by her desire to guide others to their fullest potential, Jhiree thrives on the opportunities offered by new encounters. Accomplishing goals, stacking plans and flexible contingencies, this determined professional is driven to reveal the freedom in believing that life's disadvantages do not define who we are! And through life's pains, we discover our purpose...

Current Successes

In an effort to promote the importance of Self-Care in my community, I founded an annual conference titled, "Invest in You!" This conference focuses on the importance of living a fulfilled lifestyle. I introduce participants to the benefits of practicing mindfulness, organizing their finances, and realizing the importance of nutrition and manifestation.

A second initiative that I founded is the "Rise Beyond Your Circumstance" scholarship fundraiser. Money raised is donated to Paterson High School students whose parents are substance abusers or alcoholics.

As we know, parents play a pivotal role in academia. A lack thereof causes a significant amount of emotional distress and unfortunately a devaluation of one's own self-worth. It is my goal to empower these students and raise money to provide them with some financial assistance. Having suffered this traumatic experience myself, it has become my passion to prove to these students that they have the potential to be college graduates.

Allow your circumstance to rebuild your stance!

At an early age I learned that life wouldn't be easy. Being the child of a substance abuser came with many disadvantages. I am grateful for this awareness as I discovered that when things are given to you, there's no struggle behind it. Thus, the personal connection and gratitude for it suffers.

At times, I wanted to give up on ever living a "normal" lifestyle. The idea seemed too farfetched. But, for some reason, my goals and ambitions would not allow me to quit. I desired greater things and believed I served a bigger purpose in life—for I believed that I was much more than my circumstance, my mother's addiction!

See, a circumstance is *not* something you choose; it is a situation that occurs without your permission or influence. However, your reaction to it either maintains your inner peace or causes an emotional influx.

Since life thought it awesome to throw challenges at me, I took control. I began to welcome these challenges, rather than fear them. I started to identify life as a puzzle. In every phase of my life, I'd find a different piece. All the pieces were connected, and when combined, would equate to my life story. I'll repeat that: would equate to *my life story*!

I learned to see the glass as half full. Though I viewed my experiences surrounding my mother's addiction as difficult roadblocks, I chose to turn them into challenges and check points. This positive spin allowed me to see past my circumstance.

Observe your circumstance from a position that is in your favor! Identify its purpose and choose to come out stronger on the other side!

Made in the USA
Las Vegas, NV
21 December 2020

14284068R00111